FINANCE IN THE NEW AGE

DR. JANKI MISTRY

Contents

Preface

The world has changed drastically in the last few years. Technology has grown at an unprecedented rate taking over so many aspects of our existence. The financial sector has been ambushed by the technology avalanche. This has led to an amalgam of financial theories and technology. The financial sector which had remained traditional for centuries has now become tech oriented. Technology has become an all-pervasive part of the sector. The book is a collection of short essays and reviews on the contemporary topics in finance.

Blockchain technology brought on electronic ledgers that led to rise and advent of digital and electronically encrypted currency such as Bitcoins, Ethereum among many others. Global warming and climate change has made the world aware of the green technology and hence green finance. Innovative business models and platform thinking have brought about changes in the four basic finance functions. The investment function of finance is being reinvented with concepts such as crowd funding, angel investments, venture capital and private equity. Microfinance has led the small and medium scale sector in India to new heights. Small entrepreneurs are able to get easy finance at competitive rates because of a slew of microfinance institutes across the country. Banking has become completely tech dependent with the fintech sector now growing at an unprecedented rate. The BASEL Accords have played a major role in regulating the banking sector and keeping the banks healthy. New reforms in the taxation system in terms of Goods and Services Tax has made the tax regime extremely simple and convenient for businesses. Innovative instruments of investments such as alternate investment funds and reverse mortgage investments are taking hold of the Indian investment markets. AIFs are funds that invest in promising start-ups of the country. Islamic finance products are a rage in middle eastern and certain Islamic economies. The concept of Islamic finance is like the old shirt wrapped in a new packet. Its an interesting topic and ought to be understood in order to cater to the growing Islamic population of the world as their religion doesn't allow them to take any form of interest on their investments. The role of foreign direct investment is a very important one for the growth of the country. This has been discussed in detail in one of the chapters. And lastly, the impact of the Russia-Ukraine war on the Indian economy as well as the world has been discussed.

The book is a must read for students who are pursuing higher education in management, business studies, economics or finance. It provides a basic conceptual explanation on these emerging issues in Finance.

CHAPTER I

Cryptocurrency and the Future of Money

Ms. Bhakti Jain, Ms. Hetvi Jariwala, Mr. Tapan Jariwala, Ms. Simran Lulla, Ms. Shifani Motani

1. INTRODUCTION

(What Is Bitcoin and How Does It Work? – Forbes Advisor INDIA, 25/ 03/2022)

1. History

David Chaum presented a research paper in 1983 in which he introduced the concept of digital cash. Based on his research, he founded the Digicash company in Amsterdam in 1990, which was an electronic cash company with the goal of commercialising his idea. The idea did not take off, and Chaum was forced to declare bankruptcy in 1998. Wei Dai was a software engineer and encryption expert. He holds numerous patents related to cryptographic research and inventions. Pay Pal first appeared in 1998, followed by others such as E-Gold. E-gold was backed by physical gold. It enabled members to purchase gold and silver in electronic form and make instant transfers to others. E-gold was banned because it was used by criminals and for money laundering. Wei Dai published his concept of B money in 1998. B money was intended to be an anonymous electronic cash system based on a distributed ledger. The paper possessed all of the current Cryptocurrency properties. Wei Dai described it as a system of untraceable digital transactions that allowed pseudonyms to transact with one another and enforce payments or contracts amongst themselves without outside interference. Bitcoins were inspired by Wai Dai's B-Money and incorporated its core concepts.

Liberty Reserve first appeared in 2006. Users could convert dollars or euros to liberty reserve dollars and exchange them freely for a small fee. Because it aided in money laundering, the US government shut it down. QQ Coins first appeared in 2006. One Q coin was worth one RMB and could be used to play the game or purchase merchandise. It became extremely popular in China. The whole point of all of this was to remain anonymous and out of sight of the government. This prompted Satoshi Nakamoto to create the Bitcoin cryptocurrency. It first appeared in 2008. The creator of Bitcoins initiated the system of pseudo-anonymous transactions under the pseudonym Satoshi Nakamoto, and no one knows the identity of this person or group of people who introduced Bitcoin technology to the world (Tadvi, 2018).

1.2. Architecture

Cryptocurrency is created collectively by an entire cryptocurrency system at a rate that is defined when the system is created and is publicly stated. Corporate boards or governments control the supply of currency in centrally planned banking and economic systems such as the US Federal Reserve System. Companies or governments cannot create new units of cryptocurrency and have not yet provided backing for other firms, banks, or corporate entities that hold asset value measured in it. Satoshi Nakamoto created the underlying technical system on which cryptocurrencies are based.

A community of mutually distrusting parties known as miners maintains the safety, integrity, and balance of ledgers in a proof-of-work system such as Bitcoin. Transactions in a proof-of-stake blockchain are validated by holders of the associated cryptocurrency, who are sometimes grouped together in stake pools.

Most cryptocurrencies are designed to gradually reduce the currency's production, putting a limit on the total amount of that currency that will ever be in circulation (Pagliery, 2014).

Blockchain:

A blockchain ensures the legitimacy of each cryptocurrency's coins. A blockchain is a constantly growing list of records known as blocks that are linked and secured with cryptography. Each block typically contains a hash pointer, a timestamp, and transaction data as a link to the previous block. A blockchain is typically managed as a distributed ledger by a peer-to-peer network that follows a protocol for validating new blocks. Once recorded, the data in any given block cannot be changed retroactively without affecting all subsequent blocks, which requires network majority agreement.

Blockchains are designed to be secure, and they are an example of a distributed computing system with high Byzantine fault tolerance.

Nodes: When a transaction is initiated, the node initiating the transaction broadcasts details of the transaction to other nodes throughout the node network using encryption, ensuring that the transaction (and every other transaction) is known.

Node owners are either volunteers, those hosted by the organisation or body in charge of developing the cryptocurrency blockchain network technology, or those enticed to host a node in order to receive rewards for hosting the node network.

Timestamping:

Various timestamping schemes are used by cryptocurrency to "prove" the validity of transactions added to the blockchain ledger without the need for a trusted third party.

The proof-of-work scheme was the first timestamping scheme invented. The most common proof-of-work schemes are SHA-256 and scrypt.

CryptoNight, Blake, SHA-3, and X11 are some other hashing algorithms used for proof-of-work.

The proof-of-stake scheme is another method. Some cryptocurrencies employ a hybrid proof-of-work/proof-of-stake scheme.

Mining:

Source: (Nathan, 2019)

Mining is the process of validating transactions on a blockchain. Since the introduction of Bitcoin in 2009, there has been an arms race for cheaper yet efficient machines.

As more people enter the virtual currency world, generating hashes for validation has become more complex, forcing miners to invest increasingly large sums of money to improve computing performance. By July 2019, Bitcoin's electricity consumption was estimated to be around 7 gigatonnes, or 0.2% of the global total, or the equivalent of Switzerland's national energy consumption.

Some miners pool their resources, sharing their processing power across a network, in order to split the reward equally based on the amount of work they contributed to the probability of finding a block. A "share" is given to mining pool members who present a valid partial proof-of-work.

As of February 2018, the Chinese government had halted virtual currency trading, prohibited initial coin offerings, and shut down mining. According to a February 2018 Fortune report, Iceland has become a haven for cryptocurrency miners, thanks in part to its cheap electricity.

In order to preserve natural resources and the city's "character and direction," the city of Plattsburgh, New York, imposed an 18-month moratorium on all cryptocurrency mining in March 2018.

• *GPU price increase:* In 2017, demand for graphics cards (GPU) increased due to an increase in cryptocurrency mining. Nvidia's GTX 1060 and GTX 1070 graphics cards, as well as AMD's RX 570 and RX 580 GPUs, have doubled or tripled in price, or are out of stock. Miners routinely purchase the entire stock of new GPUs as soon as they become available.

Nvidia has asked retailers to do everything possible to sell GPUs to gamers rather than miners.

Wallets:

Source: (*What Is a Crypto Wallet?, 2021*)

A cryptocurrency wallet stores the public and private "keys" (addresses) or seeds that can be used to receive or spend cryptocurrency. These methods include using paper wallets (public, private, or seed keys written on paper), hardware wallets (hardware to store your wallet information), digital wallets (computers with software hosting your wallet information), hosting your wallet on an exchange where cryptocurrency is traded, or storing your wallet information on a digital medium such as plaintext.

Anonymity:

The cryptocurrency in a wallet is not associated with a specific person, but with one or more specific keys (or "addresses"). Nonetheless, cryptocurrency exchanges are frequently required by law to collect their users' personal information.

Some cryptocurrencies, such as Monera, Zero Coin, Zero Cash, and Crypto Note, use additional privacy measures, such as zero-knowledge proofs (Pagliery, 2014).

2. DEFINITION

• There is no need for a central authority; the system's state is maintained through distributed consensus. • The system keeps track of cryptocurrency units and their ownership.

•The system governs the creation of new cryptocurrency units. If new cryptocurrency units can be created, the system defines the circumstances surrounding their creation as well as how to determine who owns these new units.

• Ownership of cryptocurrency units can be proven solely cryptographically, and the system allows transactions in which ownership of the cryptographic units is changed. Only an entity proving current ownership of these units can issue a transaction statement.

• If two different instructions for changing the ownership of the same cryptographic units are entered at the same time, the system will only execute one of them.

3. ECONOMICS

3.1. Block rewards

Proof-of-work cryptocurrencies, such as Bitcoin, provide block rewards to miners as an incentive. There has been an implicit belief that whether miners are paid through block rewards or transaction fees has no effect on blockchain security, but a study suggests that this may not be the case under certain conditions.

Miners' rewards increase the supply of cryptocurrency. Miners must not only consider the costs of the expensive equipment required to solve a hash problem, but they must also consider the significant amount of electrical power required to find the solution. In general, block rewards outweigh the costs of electricity and equipment, but this is not always the case.

The cryptocurrency's current value, rather than its long-term value, supports the reward scheme designed to encourage miners to engage in costly mining activities. According to some sources, the current Bitcoin design is extremely inefficient, resulting in a 1.4% welfare loss when compared to an efficient cash system. Carlsten and colleagues (2016)

3.2. Transaction fees

Transaction fees for cryptocurrencies are primarily determined by the availability of network capacity at the time versus the currency holder's desire for a faster transaction. The currency holder can select a transaction fee, and network entities process transactions in the order of highest offered fee to lowest offered fee. Cryptocurrency exchanges can help currency holders by providing priority options and determining which fee will most likely result in the transaction being processed in the requested time.

Transaction fees for Ether vary depending on computational complexity, bandwidth usage, and storage requirements, whereas Bitcoin transaction fees vary depending on transaction size and whether the transaction uses SegWit.

3.3. Exchanges

The availability of network capacity at the time versus the currency holder's desire for a faster transaction determines cryptocurrency transaction fees. The currency holder can choose a transaction fee, and network entities process transactions from the highest to the lowest offered fee. Currency exchanges can assist currency holders by providing priority options and determining which fee is most likely to result in the transaction being processed within the specified time frame.

Transaction fees for Ether vary according to computational complexity, bandwidth usage, and storage requirements, whereas transaction fees for Bitcoin vary according to transaction size and whether the transaction uses SegWit.

3.4. Atomic swaps

Atomic swaps are a mechanism that allows one cryptocurrency to be exchanged directly for another without the use of a trusted third party, such as an exchange.

3.5 ATMs.

Source: (*Unocoin Rolls Back First Crypto ATM in India Amidst Controversy*, 2018)

On February 20, 2014, Jordan Kelley, the founder of Robocoin, opened the first Bitcoin ATM in the United States. The kiosk, which was installed in Austin, Texas, is similar to bank ATMs but includes scanners that read government-issued identification such as a driver's licence or passport to confirm users' identities.

3.6. Initial coin offerings

An initial coin offering (ICO) is a contentious method of funding a new cryptocurrency venture. During an ICO campaign, a percentage of the cryptocurrency (usually in the form of "tokens") is sold to early project backers in exchange for legal tender or other cryptocurrencies, most commonly Bitcoin or Ether.

According to PricewaterhouseCoopers, four of the top ten proposed initial coin offerings have been registered in Switzerland as non-profit foundations. According to the Swiss regulatory agency FINMA, it will take a "balanced approach" to ICO projects, allowing "legitimate innovators to navigate the regulatory landscape and thus launch their projects in a way consistent with national laws protecting investors and the integrity of the financial system."

3.7. Price trends

A cryptocurrency's market capitalization is calculated by multiplying the price by the number of coins in circulation. Bitcoin has historically dominated the total cryptocurrency market cap, accounting for at least 50% of the market cap value, while altcoins have increased and decreased in market cap value in relation to Bitcoin. Bitcoin's value is largely determined by speculation, as well as other technological limiting factors known as blockchain rewards, which are coded into Bitcoin's architecture technology. The cryptocurrency market cap follows a trend known as "halving," which occurs when block rewards from Bitcoin are halved due to technologically mandated limited factors instilled in Bitcoin, thereby limiting the supply of Bitcoin. As the date approaches a halving (which has happened twice in history), the cryptocurrency market cap rises, followed by a downward trend.

By June 2021, some wealth managers in the United States were offering cryptocurrency for 401(k)s.

3.8. Volatility

Cryptocurrency prices are far more volatile than traditional financial assets like stocks. In May 2022, for example, Bitcoin lost 20% of its value, Ethereum lost 26%, and Solana and Cardano lost 41% and 35%, respectively. The drops were attributed to inflationary warnings. In comparison, the Nasdaq tech stock index fell 7.6% in the same week, while the FTSE 100 fell 3.6%.In the longer term, of the 10 leading cryptocurrencies identified by the total value of coins in circulation in January 2018, only four (Bitcoin, Ethereum, Cardano and Ripple (XRP)) were still in that position in early 2022. The total value of all cryptocurrencies was $2 trillion at the end of 2021, but had halved nine months later.

The Wall Street Journal has commented that the crypto sector has become "intertwined" with the rest of the capital markets and "sensitive to the same forces that drive tech stocks and other risk assets", such as inflation forecasts.

3.9. Databases

Outside of blockchains, there are also centralised databases that store crypto market data. Databases are faster than blockchains because there is no verification process. CoinMarketCap, CoinGecko, BraveNewCoin, and Cryptocompare are four of the most popular cryptocurrency market databases. 2022 (Vidal-Tomás)

4. LEGALITY

Another 15 countries have a "implicit ban," including Bahrain, Bangladesh, China, Colombia, the Dominican Republic, Indonesia, Iran, Kuwait, Lesotho, Lithuania, Macau, Oman, Qatar, Saudi Arabia, and Taiwan. State and provincial securities regulators in the United States and Canada are investigating "Bitcoin scams" and ICOs in 40 jurisdictions, coordinated through the North American Securities Administrators Association.

Bitcoin has been classified differently by various government agencies, departments, and courts. In early 2014, the China Central Bank prohibited financial institutions in China from dealing with Bitcoins.

Though cryptocurrency ownership is legal in Russia, residents arc only permitted to purchase goods from other residents using Russian rubles, whereas nonresidents are permitted to use foreign currency. Regulations and bans that apply to Bitcoin are likely to apply to other cryptocurrency systems as well.

The Bank of Thailand announced plans to launch its own cryptocurrency, the Central Bank Digital Currency, in August 2018. (CBDC). (2017, Bitcoin Value Exceeds $1 Billion as Japan and Russia Move to Legalize Cryptocurrency)

5. INCREASING REGULATIONS

The growing popularity of cryptocurrencies, as well as their adoption by financial institutions, has prompted some governments to consider whether regulation is required to protect users. The Financial Action Task Force (FATF) has classified cryptocurrency-related services as "virtual asset service providers" (VASPs) and advised that they be subject to the same anti-money laundering (AML) and know your customer (KYC) regulations as financial institutions.

The Joint Working Group on interVASP Messaging Standards published "IVMS 101" in May 2020, which is a universal common language for communicating required originator and beneficiary information between VASPs. As the data model was being developed, the FATF and financial regulators were kept informed.

The FATF updated its guidance in June 2020 to include the "Travel Rule" for cryptocurrencies, which requires VASPs to obtain, hold, and exchange information about the originators and beneficiaries of virtual asset transfers. The IVMS 101 data model has yet to be finalised and ratified by the three global standard-setting bodies that created it as of December 2020.

In September 2020, the European Commission published a digital finance strategy. This included a draught Markets in Crypto-Assets (MiCA) regulation, which aimed to provide a comprehensive regulatory framework for digital assets in the EU.

The Basel Committee on Banking Supervision proposed on June 10, 2021, that banks holding cryptocurrency assets set aside capital to cover all potential losses. Tobias Adrian, the IMF's financial counsellor and head of its monetary and capital markets department, stated in a January 2022 interview, "Agreeing on global regulations is never easy.

5.1. United States

In 2021, 17 states passed cryptocurrency-related legislation and resolutions. The Securities and Exchange Commission (SEC) of the United States is debating what steps to take. Senator Elizabeth Warren, a member of the Senate Banking Committee, wrote to the chairman of the SEC on July 8, 2021, demanding that it provide answers on cryptocurrency regulation by July 28, 2021, [needs update] due to the increased use of cryptocurrency exchanges and the risk this poses to consumers. On February 17, 2022, the Justice Department appointed Eun Young Choi as the first director of a National Cryptocurrency Enforcement Team to assist in the identification and resolution of cryptocurrencies and other digital assets misuse.

5.2. China

In September 2017, China prohibited ICOs from causing abnormal returns on cryptocurrency during the announcement window. The liquidity changes caused by China's ICO ban were initially negative, but the liquidity effect turned positive after the news.

China banned financial institutions and payment companies from providing cryptocurrency transaction services on May 18, 2021. As a result, the price of the largest proof of work cryptocurrencies fell precipitously. For example, Bitcoin fell 31%, Ethereum 44%, Binance Coin 32%, and Dogecoin 30%.

5.3. India

At the moment, neither India prohibits nor permits investment in the cryptocurrency market. The Reserve Bank of India's ban on cryptocurrency was lifted by the Supreme Court of India in 2020. Since then, cryptocurrency investment has been considered legal, though there is still ambiguity regarding the extent and payment of tax on income derived from it, as well as its regulatory regime. However, it is expected that the Indian Parliament will soon pass legislation to either ban or regulate the cryptocurrency market in India. A leading public policy lawyer and Vice President of SAARCLAW (South Asian Association for Regional Cooperation in Law) Hemant Batra stated to a well-known online publication that the "cryptocurrency market has now become very big with involvement of billions of dollars in the market thus, it is now unattainable and irreconcilable for the government to completely ban all types of cryptocurrency." He proposed regulating the cryptocurrency market rather than outright prohibiting it. In this regard, he advocated for adhering to IMF and FATF guidelines. (From Ban to Regulation: A Look at the Cryptocurrency Journey in India, 2021)

6. CRITICISM

Eight Nobel Laureates in Economic Sciences, including Paul Krugman and Robert J. Rubin, as well as central bank officials such as Alan Greenspan, Agustin Carstens, Vitor Constâncio, and NoutWellink, have described Bitcoin as a speculative bubble.

The investors Warren Buffett and George Soros have respectively characterised it as a "mirage" and a "bubble"; Morgan Chase CEO Jamie Dimon have called it a "bubble" and a "fraud", respectively, although Jamie Dimon later said he regretted dubbing Bitcoin a fraud. Bitcoin has been dubbed a "index of money laundering" by Fink.

Bill Gates stated in June 2022 that cryptocurrencies are "100% based on greater fool theory." (News, 2018)

7. SOCIAL TRENDS

According to Alan Feuer of The New York Times, libertarians and anarcho-capitalists were drawn to Bitcoin's philosophical concept. Economist Paul Krugman claims that cryptocurrencies such as Bitcoin are a "cult" based on "paranoid fantasies" about government power.

In the social life of Bitcoin, Nigel Dodd argues that the essence of the Bitcoin ideology is to remove money from both social and governmental control. Dodd talks about the ""Declaration of Bitcoin's Independence," a crypto-anarchist message that states: "Bitcoin is inherently anti-establishment, anti-system, and anti-state. Because Bitcoin is fundamentally humanitarian, it undermines governments and disrupts institutions."

According to David Golumbia, the ideas influencing Bitcoin advocates are influenced by right-wing extremist movements such as the Liberty Lobby and the John Birch Society and their anti-Central Bank rhetoric, or, more recently, Ron Paul and Tea Party-style libertarianism. In 2008, Nakamoto stated.

According to the European Central Bank, the decentralisation of money provided by Bitcoin has its theoretical roots in the Austrian school of economics, specifically Friedrich von Hayek's book Denationalization of Money: The Argument Refined, in which Hayek advocates a complete free market in the production, distribution, and management of money in order to end central banks' monopoly. Brito BitcoinPrimer.Pdf (Brito, 2013)

8. ADVANTAGES AND DISADVANTAGES

8.1 Advantages

Open source code for crypto currency mining

BTC employs the same algorithms used in online banking. The only difference between Internet banking and traditional banking is the disclosure of user information. The BTC network shares all transaction information (how, when), but there is no information about the recipient or sender of the coins (there is no access to the owner's wallet).

There is no inflation

The maximum number of coins is set at 21 million Bitcoins. Because neither political forces nor corporations have the ability to change this order, there is no chance of inflation developing in the system.

A cryptocurrency network that operates on a peer-to-peer basis

In such networks, there is no master server in charge of all operations. Information (in this case, money) is exchanged between 2-3 or more software clients. All program-wallets installed by users are part of the bitcoin network. Each client keeps track of all committed transactions as well as the amount of bitcoins in each wallet. Hundreds of distributed servers process transactions. Banks, taxes, and governments have no control over the exchange of money.

Transaction possibilities are limitless

Each wallet holder has the ability to pay anyone, anywhere, and in any amount. Because the transaction cannot be controlled or prevented, you can send money to anyone in the world who has a Bitcoin wallet.

There are no limits

It is not possible to cancel payments made through this system. The coins cannot be counterfeited, copied, or used twice. These capabilities ensure the overall system's integrity. Every month, the number of online stores, resources, and businesses that accept Bitcoin grows.

Low BTC operating expenses

The BTC cryptocurrency functions as physical cash, combining e-commerce functions. There is no need to pay commissions or fees to banks or other organisations. The main component of such a process is mathematics, which is free of charge. This system has the lowest commission fee of any. It equates to 0.1% of the transaction value. The operation interest charges are deposited into the wallets of Bitcoin miners.

Decentralization

The network has no centralised control authority; instead, it is distributed to all participants; each computer mining bitcoins is a member of this system. This means that the central authority has no authority to impose rules on bitcoin owners. Even if a portion of the network goes down, the payment system will remain stable.

Simple to use

Given that the procedure for opening a company account in Ukrainian banks is overly complicated and can be refused without explanation, using BTC is advantageous for businesses. The company creates a BTC wallet in about 5 minutes and immediately begins using it without any questions or commissions.

Anonymity

It is completely anonymous while also being completely transparent. Without regard for name, address, or any other information, any company can generate an infinite number of bitcoin addresses.

Transparency

The BTC keeps track of all transactions that have ever occurred. A blockchain is a sequential chain of blocks. Everything is recorded in the block chain. As a result, if the company has used the BTC address publicly, anyone can see how much BTC is owned. If the company address is not made public, no one will ever know it belongs to this company. Companies typically use a unique BTC address for each transaction to ensure complete anonymity.

Transaction speed

The ability to send money anywhere and to anyone in a matter of minutes after the payment is processed by the BTC network.

It belongs only to the wallet owner

There is a one-of-a-kind electronic payment system in which the account belongs solely to the owner. For example, if the company decides that the owner is misusing the account for any reason, the system has the authority to freeze all funds on the account without even informing the owner.

The owner is solely responsible for ensuring that the account is being used properly. The owner of BTC has a private key and a corresponding public key, which is the BTC wallet address. Bitcoins can only be withdrawn by the owner.

There are no chances of using some personal data for fraud

This is a critical point. Credit cards are now used for the vast majority of purchases. They are untrustworthy. Customers must enter the following information when filling out forms on websites: card number, expiration date, and code. It's difficult to think of a less secure method of payment. As a result, credit cards are frequently stolen. BTC transactions do not necessitate the disclosure of any personal information. It instead employs two keys: public and private. The public key is available to everyone (for example, the address of a Bitcoin wallet), but the private key is only known to the owner. The transaction must be signed by using interacting private keys and a mathematical function. This establishes that the transaction was carried out by the owner. (n.d., Cryptocurrencies.Pdf)

8.2. Disadvantages

According to above mentioned author, Ivaschenko (2016) the disadvantages are as follows:

High volatility

Almost all of the ups and downs in the BTC value are directly related to government declarations from various countries. In the short term, this volatility causes a problem.

Investing in cryptocurrency carries significant risks

In our opinion, the list of cryptocurrencies' (bitcoin) disadvantages is much longer, and is related to the risk of money laundering, terrorist and other illegal activity financing, the lack of a central issuer, which means there is no legal formal entity to guaranty in the event of a bankruptcy, and so on. Although it is difficult to predict, many academics and professionals in this field believe that the future of cryptocurrencies is bright because it will remove trade barriers and intermediaries, reduce transaction costs, and thus boost trade and the economy. Nonetheless, we should consider and pessimistic voices in the academic world, who suggest that the high risk of volatility, hacking risks, and a lack of institutional backup make the future of cryptocurrencies not very hopeful. (n.d., Cryptocurrencies.Pdf).

References:

Bitcoin value rises over $1 billion as Japan, Russia move to legitimize cryptocurrency. (n.d.). Retrieved November 25, 2022, from https://www.cnbc.com/2017/04/12/bitcoin-price-rises-japan-russia-regulation.html

Brito_BitcoinPrimer.pdf. (n.d.). Retrieved November 25, 2022, from https://www.mercatus.org/system/files/Brito_BitcoinPrimer.pdf

Carlsten, M., Kalodner, H., Weinberg, S. M., & Narayanan, A. (2016). On the Instability of Bitcoin Without the Block Reward. *Proceedings of the 2016 ACM SIGSAC Conference on Computer and Communications Security*, 154–167. https://doi.org/10.1145/2976749.2978408

Cryptocurrencies.pdf. (n.d.). Retrieved November 25, 2022, from https://eprints.ugd.edu.mk/18707/1/Cryptocurrencies.pdf

Current Cryptocurrency Regulations in India | Coinpedia. (n.d.). Retrieved November 25, 2022, from https://coinpedia.org/cryptocurrency-regulation/cryptocurrency-regulations-in-india/

Database change management—Kamil Grzybek. (n.d.). Retrieved November 25, 2022, from http://www.kamilgrzybek.com/database/database-change-management/

From ban to regulation: A look at the journey of cryptocurrencies in India. (n.d.). Retrieved November 25, 2022, from https://indianexpress.com/article/technology/crypto/cryptocurrency-in-india-a-look-at-the-regulatory-journey-of-cryptocurrencies-7648767/

News, E. C. O. (2018, January 22). *Economics Nobel prize winner, Richard Thaler: "The market that looks most like a bubble to me is Bitcoin and its brethren."* ECO News. https://econews.pt/2018/01/22/economics-nobel-prize-winner-richard-thaler-the-market-that-looks-most-like-a-bubble-to-me-is-bitcoin-and-its-brethren/

Pagliery, J. (2014). *Bitcoin: And the Future of Money*. Triumph Books.

Shodhganga@INFLIBNET: A look at the sinister connection between money laundering and crypto currencies and the laws governing them. (n.d.). Retrieved November 17, 2022, from https://shodhganga.inflibnet.ac.in/handle/10603/257334

Unocoin Rolls Back First Crypto ATM in India Amidst Controversy. (2018, October 24). CCN.Com. https://www.ccn.com/unocoin-rolls-back-first-crypto-atm-in-india-amidst-controversy/

Vidal-Tomás, D. (2022). Which cryptocurrency data sources should scholars use? *International Review of Financial Analysis, 81*, 102061. https://doi.org/10.1016/j.irfa.2022.102061

What Is a Crypto Wallet? A Beginner's Guide – N26. (n.d.). Retrieved November 25, 2022, from https://n26.com/en-eu/blog/what-is-a-crypto-wallet

What Is Bitcoin and How Does It Work? – Forbes Advisor INDIA. (n.d.). Retrieved November 25, 2022, from https://www.forbes.com/advisor/in/investing/cryptocurrency/what-is-bitcoin-and-how-does-it-work/

CHAPTER II

Fintech Startups in India

Ms. Shruti Asmaniwala, Ms. Priyal Chhogani, Mr. Chirag Gadhvi, Mr. Sameer Noorani, Mr. Krunal Parmar, Mr. Shiv Burkhawala

1. INTRODUCTION TO FINTECH

1. FinTech firms are those that provide economically viable applications of technology to financial services or products. Payments, Lending, Wealth Technology (WealthTech), Personal Finance Management, Insurance Technology (InsurTech), Regulation Technology (RegTech), and other segments comprise India's FinTech companies (Akansha, 2022).
2. **FinTech Ecosystem**

The various participants in a FinTech Ecosystem and how they are interconnected with FinTech solution providers:

- *Investors:* Venture capitalists, angel investors, and private equity firms view FinTech companies as the next golden goose.
- *Traditional Financial Institutions:* Banks and financial service providers are creating ways to engage with FinTech in order to take advantage of the technological revolution and cut operational expenses.
- *Government and Regulators:* Appropriate regulations safeguard end users and establish limitations for FinTech to operate inside.
- *Universities and Research Institutions:* In India, institutes with a curriculum that focuses on FinTech enterprises are addressing the severe scarcity of skilled and well-trained workers.
- *Incubators:* Several established companies in India are establishing incubators for FinTech in order to test and expand their services.
- *Users:* The end user remains the most essential component of FinTech. Increased usage and acceptance by Indians pave the path for the establishment of additional FinTech enterprises in India.

1. RECENT DEVELOPMENTS AND TRENDS IN THE FINTECH SECTOR

- ***Block chain:*** Block chain technology has radically altered the FinTech industry's mode of operation. This cutting-edge technology makes it possible to conduct transactions in a safe and secure manner. As a result, banks and financial institutions are rapidly adopting Block chain technology to capitalise on its advantages.
- Block chain ensures that the stored information is protected end-to-end with minimal risk. Block chain is also used to assure the security of international transactions.
- ***Artificial Intelligence and Machine Learning:*** Intelligent algorithms enhance a variety of banking, credit, and insurance procedures. The behaviour of ordinary banking application users is "studied" using artificial intelligence. If a fraudster gains access to the platform, artificial intelligence detects abnormal behaviour and notifies the client and the bank of the danger. Intelligent virtual assistants are built using AI. These are chatbots that assist consumers with problem resolution 24/7. The system analyses user behaviour and provides customised financial advise with more advantageous conditions for the client.

- ***Biometric Authentication:*** Biometric authentication is regarded as more secure than traditional passwords and PINs. Users despise having to remember several passwords and view biometric authentication as the superior method of identity verification. They are not required to recall combinations of letters and numbers; passwords are changed annually. Even if your mobile device or laptop is taken, confidential data will remain secure. FinTech is becoming a key industry for biometric authentication technology as 93% of consumers regard the protection of financial accounts to be the most essential concern.
- ***Open Banking:*** Open API, or open banking, is based on releasing bank customer data to third parties with the owner's permission. This information transmission style is advantageous for bank customers.
- Thanks to open API, the bank shares the client's financial information with insurance providers, retailers, and other organisations. Prior to offering insurance, a loan, or permitting payment in instalments, they must verify the client's financial stability. Open banking is altering the market, allowing customers to make online purchases in a few simple steps, pay for services with a single swipe, and obtain a loan in a matter of seconds.

- *The Internet of Things:* FinTech firms are increasingly employing linked gadgets to collect business-friendly customer insights and make better educated judgements. The market for wearables will expand from $48.89 billion in 2021 to $118.16 billion in 2028 due to the rising interest in IoT. Connected wearables perform several useful activities in FinTech, including mobile banking applications, financial institutions monitoring client behaviour to determine what services to offer, and mobile point-of-sale (POS) systems replacing conventional POS systems. Smartphones, bracelets, and smartwatches are utilised as payment alternatives to credit cards, while connected speakers and smart refrigerators order and pay for their own supplies.
- *Robotic Process Automation:* A "Robot" inputs data, generates reports, maintains financial information, verifies the solvency of a bank's client, handles insurance claims, manages customer requests and complaints, and registers consumers. RPA is the key to the success of FinTech, forecasting a 400% increase in revenue by 2023.
- RegTech is an acronym for Regulatory Technology, which refers to the technological management of the regulatory process in the financial industry. RegTech's primary functions are reporting, monitoring, and compliance.
- The proliferation of digital products has also contributed to an increase in instances of money laundering, fraudulent operations, cyber hacking, and data breaches.
- With the use of Big Data and Machine Learning, RegTech can provide vital information on money laundering operations, hence minimising the risk connected with the compliance department. In addition, RegTech can decrease administrative costs, assure financial stability, and safeguard clients. (Top FinTech Predictions and Trends for 2022, 2022) (Top Ten FinTech Trends to Watch in 2022, BFSI News, ET BFSI, FinTech)

3. ADVANTAGES AND DISADVANTAGES OF FINTECH STARTUPS

3.1 Advantages of FinTech Startups

Big Numbers of Business Opportunities: As a founder of a FinTech company, one has a tonne of inspiring business prospects that enable you to tap into your creativity. There are still a lot of financial issues that need to be resolved, and with the appropriate Eureka moment, one can come up with an excellent answer.

The Growth of Investments and the Number of Investors: FinTech investment has increased since 2010, and it has increased more quickly in nations with better regulations and greater innovation potential. The fact that more than $100 billion was invested in FinTech in 2020 alone lends support to the bullish investment claim. This demonstrates the high level of investor confidence in the industry, which increases the likelihood that a notable innovation will receive crucial financial assistance.

It's also important to understand that founders are not restricted in how much money they can raise in a single investment round. For instance, the Chinese FinTech business Ant Financial raised $14 billion in a single fundraising round. This is an excellent illustration of the amount of investment available for fintech firms.

InsurTech is Making Giant Strides: The entire FinTech sector is experiencing tremendous growth. However, InsurTech is a standout shining light in the illuminating sector. Despite being a distinct business, InsurTech is frequently considered a subset of FinTech.

As the name suggests, insurtech involves the use of Big Data and artificial intelligence to process a person's medical and criminal histories wherever it is allowed by law. To lower startup risk and recommend the best choice to an insurance policy customer, it also looks at open social media information, credit history, and other data.

For those looking for an industry that may promise rapid growth, this area is widely regarded as a founders' paradise. How? Over the next seven years, experts predict that InsurTech will easily grow into the next enormous FinTech sub-sector, with a mind-blowing CAGR of 48.8 percent (Benefits of FinTech for Businesses and Startups [and More], 2021).

3.2 Disadvantages of FinTech Startups

Regulatory and Compliance Laws: The delay of FinTech start-ups in the Indian financial sector is a result of numerous restrictions. These rules are difficult to follow, and they also make it difficult for FinTech companies to join the Indian markets. In order to combat fraud, compliance regulations are put in place as a stringent regulatory framework. However, they too serve as significant obstacles for the new FinTech players. Before they even begin operations, FinTech start-ups must complete a long number of requirements.

Unbanked and under banked Population: FinTech's initial growth was sluggish because to weak infrastructures, such as low internet penetration and low literacy rates in India. Although the Indian government is addressing these problems with generous policies, the advantages won't become apparent for some time.

Trust in Cash: When it comes to daily transactions, the majority of Indians take a conservative stance and settle on utilising cash. They have relied on money as a sales medium for a very long time, thus it is challenging for them to break their habits and adopt new strategies. It is challenging to offer financial services in an unbanked market because these services are frequently connected to online fraud. Due to their lack of financial literacy, many Indians are unable to recognise the value that FinTech offers through its cutting-edge goods and services.

Cyber threats: FinTech businesses handle private client information. Online transactions suffer significant monetary losses as a result of numerous cyber security vulnerabilities. These are completely unjustified for the customers. The same technology that makes life more convenient also makes it easier for thieves to access people's internet accounts. This is a continuous flow that contributes to FinTech's appeal. FinTech must protect itself from any threats put out by hackers. Digitally accessible financial information on people and businesses is enormous. The likelihood of cyber security breaches rises as a result.

Industry-Related Complexities: FinTech are made to function with a complex operating model. They find it challenging to keep good ties with other financial institutions like banks as a result. However, banks are hesitant to collaborate with FinTech because they fear harming their reputation. 6 Major Obstacles for Indian FinTech Startups, according to the Finezza Blog, 2022.

4. INDIA TOWARDS BECOMING THE GLOBAL FINTECH SUPERPOWER

The rate of worldwide adoption of fintech is highest in India.

One of the world's FinTech marketplaces with the quickest growth rates is India. In India, there are already more than 2,000 recognised Financial Technology (FinTech) startups.

Market size for the Indian FinTech sector is expected to reach $50 billion in 2021 and $150 billion by 2025.

By 2023, it is anticipated that India's FinTech industry would have $1 trillion in assets under management (AUM) and $200 billion in revenue.

The most popular sectors were payments, lending, and insurtech.

From January 2017 to July 2022, the Indian FinTech market attracted $29 billion in funding across 2,084 agreements, garnering a 14% share of worldwide funding and ranking second in terms of deal volume.

In FY22, $8.53 billion (in 278 deals) was invested in the FinTech business in India.

India has 23 FinTech startups that, as of July 2022, have achieved "Unicorn Status" with a valuation of more than $1 billion.

According to data from the Financial Services Sector in India | FinTech Industry in India from April 2022, 358 banks were participating in India's Unified Payments Interface (UPI) as of September 2022, and there were 6.8 billion transactions totaling more than $135 billion.

The Role of FinTech Companies in India Towards Reshaping the Financial Services Landscape

High costs are the main obstacle to traditional banking, leaving the majority of the population under or not banked. By removing costly physical networks, outmoded legacy processes, IT systems, and operational models, fintech is here to disrupt that.

The offerings and service fees in the traditional banking ecosystem have been remarkably similar. FinTech offers a range of service diversification and personalization options to accommodate various social strata.

Utilizing cutting-edge technology like blockchain, artificial intelligence, and big data analytics, Indian FinTech companies have created sophisticated methodologies for risk assessment. To reach out to rural places, the credit requirement situation can be altered.

The goals of fintech innovation are to develop superior financial products, improve the client experience, and boost transparency.

5. GROWTH DRIVERS OF FINTECH STARTUPS

Volume of Funds: Innovation in the industry is being driven by a large amount of money from institutional investors, private equity, and venture capital.

India stack: Aadhar, UPI, Bharat Bill Payments, and GSTRILLION are examples of open API systems.

Technological Innovation: putting into practise innovative business models that are driven by AI and machine learning technology.

Increasing internet & Smartphone penetration: India is the second-largest market for Internet users and already has the second-highest number of smartphone users worldwide. 1 Billion People Will Be Online by 2026. By 2026, there will be 233 million households with internet connections, up from 160 million in 2021. This is a 46% increase.

Favorable Demographics: In 2020, there were 68 percent of young people in India, and by 2025, it is predicted that 56 percent of the country's population will be in the working age range of 20 to 59. India will add 140 million middle-class and 21 million high-income families by 2030, which would fuel demand for and growth in the country's fintech industry.

Financial Inclusion Initiatives: Programs for financial inclusion like PMJDY, DAY-NRLM, Direct Benefit Transfer, and Atal Pension Yojana, among others, have sped up the digital revolution and expanded access to digital financial services for more people, particularly in rural areas (Financial Services Sector in India | FinTech Industry in India, April, 2022).

References:

6 Key Challenges That Fintech Startups Face in India—Finezza Blog. (2022). Retrieved November 17, 2022, from https://finezza.in/blog/6-key-challenges-that-fintech-startups-face-in-india/

Benefits of FinTech for Businesses and Startups [and more]. (2021). Retrieved November 17, 2022, from https://spdload.com/blog/benefits-of-fintech/

Financial Services Sector in India | Fintech Industry in India. (April, 2022). Retrieved November 17, 2022, from https://www.investindia.gov.in/sector/bfsi-fintech-financial-services

FinTech in 2022: Top predictions and trends. (2022). Retrieved November 17, 2022, from https://www.digipay.guru/blog/top-fintech-predictions-trends/

Fintech: Top ten FinTech trends to watch out for in 2022, BFSI News, ET BFSI. (05/13/2022). Retrieved November 17, 2022, from https://bfsi.economictimes.indiatimes.com/amp/news/fintech/top-ten-fintech-trends-to-watch-out-for-in-2022/91512668

Top challenges of Indian FinTech Companies | Valuebound. (07/27/2022). Retrieved November 17, 2022, from https://www.valuebound.com/resources/blog/top-challenges-indian-fintech-companies

CHAPTER III

Green Finance

Mr. Mikesh Gandhi, Ms. Srushti Gohil, Ms. Ankita Hirapara, Mr. Devanshu Kapadia, Mr. Meet Patel

1. INTRODUCTION:

Any structured financial activity designed to promote better environmental outcomes is referred to as "green finance."

An estimated $1 trillion per year will be needed in the near future to fund the transition to a low-carbon economy, which is why green finance is becoming more and more popular in the UK and around the world. This creates a huge opportunity for the financial services industry, both commercially and in terms of the sector's ability to demonstrate its social mission by aiding in the transition to a low-carbon, sustainable society.

The phrase "green economy" was originally used in a 1989 report for the government of the United Kingdom by a group of eminent environmental economists. The purpose of the report was to inform the UK government as to whether the phrase "sustainable development" had a widely accepted definition.

In slightly over 11 months in 2021, India issued over $6.11 billion in green bonds to finance initiatives that will benefit the environment and/or the climate. A negligible amount of foreign interest is anticipated in the green bond market, where we lag only behind the US and China. This is because foreign investors typically seek out risk-free procedures, a standardised tax structure, and a regulated financial infrastructure before considering a long-term investment. In order to attract green money, developing nations require a strong banking system, according to the UN Environment Programme (UNEP)(*Green Financing in India — Need, Significance, Urgency, and Way Forward | Business Insider India*, n.d.) (*6e89f43e-6a3b-41c7-A2a65d41deeee960.Pdf*, n.d.).

1. CONCEPTUAL FRAMEWORK:

2.1 Definition:

A loan or investment known as "green financing" is fundamentally one that is intended to encourage environmentally beneficial activity and can assist you in funding those improvements, occasionally even offering incentives to do so. As a result, it can assist individuals and organisations in making wise investments and purchases for both themselves and the environment.

Increased investment in clean and green technologies, financing for sustainable natural resource-based green economies and climate-smart blue economies, harmonising public financial incentives, changes to country regulatory frameworks, increased green financing from various sectors, alignment of public sector financing decision-making with the environmental dimension of the Sustainable Development Goals, and increased use of green bonds etc.

2.2 Indian context:

A loan or investment known as "green financing" is fundamentally one that is intended to encourage environmentally beneficial activity and can assist you in funding those improvements, occasionally even offering incentives to do so. As a result, it can assist individuals and organisations in making wise investments and purchases for both themselves and the environment.

Increased investment in clean and green technologies, financing for sustainable natural resource-based green economics and climate-smart blue economies, harmonising public financial incentives, changes to country regulatory frameworks, increased green financing from various sectors, alignment of public sector financing decision-making with the environmental dimension of the Sustainable Development Goals, and increased use ofIndia's green finance flows are far insufficient to meet the nation's existing needs. A fourth of India's demands, or about INR 309,000 crores (USD 44 billion) year, was met through monitored green finance in 2019/2020.

The term "green finance" refers to financial arrangements made specifically for the use of environmentally friendly projects or initiatives that incorporate climate change-related elements. Energy-efficient projects like green building, waste management that includes recycling, effective disposal, and energy conversion are all examples of environmentally sustainable initiatives. They also include clean transportation that entails decreased greenhouse gas emissions.

The whole debate of the sustainability of economic growth revolves around green finance.

2.3 Public policy towards green finance in India:

- **International best practices:**

Since the G20's inaugural summit in 2008, climate change has been a top priority, but more recently, the circular carbon economy (CCE) has received increased attention as a means of reducing harmful emissions. Global regulatory framework-focused flagship initiatives can be roughly divided into four categories.

The companies are required to report their exposure to ESG-related risks from their operations on a regular basis as part of the sustainability disclosure by financial and non-financial companies. Following the G20's encouragement of corporate voluntary acceptance of the Task Force on Climate-related Financial Disclosures' guidelines, such disclosures have increased (TCFD).

The second method is guided and concessional lending, which is present in many nations.

A further US$200 million fund was established for the leather and textile sector in order to support the industry's transition to green technologies in 2016.

Third, do financial and non-financial institutions fall under micro- and macro-prudential regulations?

The creation of green financial institutions comes in at number four. The UK Green Investment Bank plc was founded in 2012 and is a GBP 3 billion (USD 3.9 billion) enterprise owned entirely by the UK government (Geddes et al., 2018).

TABLE 1: Participation of Asian Financial Institutions in Global Initiatives

Name of the initiative	Global signatories	Asian signatories	Global Signatories	Asian Signatories
	From Volz,2020		As of the of end 2021	
Principles for Responsible Investment	1,847	122	2,698	387
Equator Principles Financial Institutions	91	12	101	22
UNEP Statement of Commitment by Financial Institutions on Sustainable Development (2011)	214	38		
Sustainable Stock Exchanges	66	14		

- **Public policy in India:**

India began emphasising green finance in 2007. The Reserve Bank of India released a notification in December 2007 on "Corporate Social Responsibility, Sustainable Development, and Non-financial Reporting - Role of Banks," which emphasises the importance of global warming and climate change in the framework of sustainable development.

In India, numerous fiscal and financial incentives have been implemented. These incentives are consistent with India's objectives under the 2015 Paris Agreement to reduce greenhouse gas emissions intensity by 33 to 35 percent below 2005 levels by 203010. In addition, the Reserve Bank has taken aggressive policy measures to encourage and support green financing activities. In 2015, it included the small renewable energy industry to its Priority Sector Lending (PSL) scheme.

Firms in the renewable energy sector13 are eligible for loans of up to 30 crores (up from '15 crores starting September 4, 2020), while families are eligible for loans of up to '10 lakh for renewable energy investment. India established a target of 450 GW of renewable energy output by 2030 in September 2019.

The Reserve Bank of India emphasised the risk of climate change on financial assets and the need to accelerate green finance for environmentally friendly sustainable development in its Report on Trend and Progress of Banking in India (2018-19). It recognises the problems in the growth of green finance, such as "greenwashing" or false claims of environmental compliance, a diversity of definitions, and maturity mismatches between long-term green investment and investors' short-term objectives. It also emphasises the need for governmental action to create a framework that promotes the green finance ecosystem in India by raising awareness through collaborative initiatives.

In terms of green financial institutions, the Indian Renewable Energy Development Agency (IREDA), a government-backed organisation that promotes renewable energy investments, revealed plans in May 2016 to become India's first green bank. The India Infrastructure Finance Corporation Limited (IIFCL) also developed a separate scheme known as the "credit enhancement scheme" to fund viable infrastructure projects with bond maturities greater than five years (Jain, 2020). In the following section, we shall analyse the growth of green financing in India, including broad understanding of environmental sustainability.(*Green Finance: 'India and Green Economy: What's the Current Status, How Banks Are Playing Their Part?, BFSI News, ET BFSI*, n.d.)

3. ADVANTAGES:

- Green funding on a large scale indicates that green or environmental efforts take precedence over traditional economic investments that may or may not be sustainable.
- Focusing on such funding results in transparency and a steady flow of investments towards environmental goals.
- The expansion of this sort of funding will contribute to the creation of new jobs and business possibilities.
- All of this will eventually lead to greater human life and amenities, as well as sustainable development that does not harm or damage nature(*Green Finance – Meaning, Benefits, Challenges and Trends | EFM*, n.d.).

4. CHALLENGES:

- Often, investors' short-term time horizons do not align with long-term green investments.
- There will always be a concern about effective coordination, cooperation, and alignment of financial and environmental goals. Each would desire to pull the trigger in order to prioritise its goals (*Green Finance – Meaning, Benefits, Challenges and Trends | EFM*, n.d.).

5. GREEN FINANCIAL PRODUCTS AND SERVICES IN INDIA:

5.1 Green bond

A green bond is a device with characteristics identical to a conventional coupon bond, with the exception that the proceeds from this bond are used in energy-efficient projects related to renewable energy, production reduction, reforestation, and so on.

In February 2014, the Indian Renewable Energy Development Agency (IRDA) launched a tax-free Green Bond for Rs.1,000 apiece. It issued bonds with durations of 10 years, 15 years, and 20 years, with interest rates of 8.16 percent, 8.55 percent, and 8.55 percent per annum, respectively. It received a AAA rating from CARE and Brick Works. Yes, in February 2015, the bank issued a 10-year Green Infrastructure bond for Rs.1,000 crores.

The bank's funds would be used to finance Green Infrastructure projects such as solar electricity, biomass, wind power, and minor hydel projects. It has partnered with KPMG India to provide annual assurance services based on the green bond standards. Yes Bank issued another green bond as a private assignment in 2016 for INR 3.15 billion, with International Finance Corporation (IFC) as the sole investor. ICRA and CARE have assigned the bond an AA+ rating. In March 2015, EXIM Bank of India issued a $500 million green bond with a maturity of five years. It is India's first green bond denominated in US dollars..

2. Green insurance

Green insurance schemes are those that offer low-cost risk coverage and increased coverage for green products in order to mitigate the effects of climate change, while encouraging good business conduct. In India, HSBC is currently collaborating with Allianz to provide green reinvestment insurance to its consumers.

It covers buildings that have been certified by international environmental standards such as the US Leadership in Energy and Environmental Design (LEED) and the Building Research Establishment Environmental Assessment Methodology (BREEAM). With only a slight premium increase, this coverage gives an additional 5% over and above the regular covered loss amount. This would incentivize builders to construct more energy-efficient structures.

3. Green loan schemes

Green loan schemes are financing programmes offered by commercial banks and financial organisations at low interest rates to encourage investment in energy-efficient projects.

State Bank of India (SBI) has launched a Green Home Bank loan scheme with low interest rates to encourage customers to choose green housing, which is defined as buildings certified by rating agencies such as Leadership in Energy & Environmental Design (LEED) India, India Green Building Council (IGBC), and TERI - GRIHA from TERI- BCSD India. ICICI Bank has launched a vehicle finance scheme that aims to reduce interest rates by 50% on loans taken by consumers for the purchase of cars that use renewable energy sources, such as Honda's Civic Hybrid, Tata Indica CNG, Reva electric cars, Mahindra Logan CNG versions, Maruti's LPG version of Maruti 800, Omni, and Versa, and Hyundai's Santro Eco. The bank seeks to cut processing fees for consumers purchasing houses in LEED-certified buildings through its Home finance programmes. (2015) (Raghupati and Sujatha) Union Bank of India has programmes that provide loans to farmers for the purchase of solar water heaters, solar water pumps, and the installation of solar house lighting systems. PNB's Saur Urja Yojna provides medium-term loan schemes to farmers for the construction of greenhouses and the establishment of biogas plants with sanitary latrines, as well as a scheme for small farmers to fund the purchase of solar home lights and water heaters. India, a developing country, has a bond market that is still in its early stages (Sustainability Initiatives in India's Financial Sector | Download Table, n.d.).

6. FUTURE SCOPE OF GREEN FINANCE IN INDIA:

Sustainability of the environment is a critical issue on a global scale, which has raised the potential for investment in green initiatives utilising renewable energy resources. As a result, numerous banks and financial organisations are eager to enter this expanding market. As a result, demand for Green bonds and structured green funds will rise.

Furthermore, investors would gain from diversification by investing in such bonds. This is also true in the context of India, as a study by Mc Kinsey & Co. discovered that a probable increase in carbon emissions to 5-6.5 million MT in India could be reduced by 30 percent to 50 percent by 2030 by investing in energy-efficient technologies in building infrastructure, and that an additional 600-750 billion Euros would be required for this purpose, even after accounting for the steep decline in the cost of renewable energy technologies. The International Finance Corporation (IFC) has already taken a move in this direction. In 2015, it chose to put $75 million into green bonds issued by Punjab National Bank Housing Finance Ltd. These are secured non-convertible debentures, the revenues of which will be used to build green residential structures certified by the World Bank's EDGE.

In India, a Council on Climate Change was established in 2007 and reformed in 2014 under the Prime Minister's supervision to address climate change adaptation and mitigation. It has launched several programmes, including the National Climate Change Action Plan, the Jawaharlal Nehru National Solar Mission, the National Water Mission, the National Mission for Enhanced Energy Efficiency, the National Mission on Strategic Knowledge for Climate Change, and the National Clean Energy Fund. Other initiatives include Auto Fuel Vision and Policy 2025, Expert Groups on Low Carbon Strategies, and so on. NABARD was recognised as a National Implementing Entity (NIE) to finance renewable energy projects in India by the Green Climate Fund, which was established under the framework of the United Nations Framework Convention on Climate Change (UNFCCC) in 2015 (*Sustainability Initiatives in the Financial Sector in India | Download Table*, n.d.).

References:

6e89f43e-6a3b-41c7-a2a65d41deeee960.pdf. (n.d.). Retrieved November 17, 2022, from https://www.charteredbanker.com/static/uploaded/ 6e89f43e-6a3b-41c7-a2a65d41deeee960.pdf

Green Finance – Meaning, Benefits, Challenges and Trends | eFM. (n.d.). Retrieved November 17, 2022, from https://efinancemanagement.com/ sources-of-finance/green-finance

Green Finance: 'India and green econom: What's the current status, how banks are playing their part?, BFSI News, ET BFSI. (n.d.). Retrieved November 17, 2022, from https://bfsi.economictimes.indiatimes.com/ amp/news/financial-services/india-and-green-economy-whats-the-current-status-how-banks-are-playing-their-part/93695172

OPINION: Green financing in India—Need, significance, urgency, and way forward | Business Insider India. (n.d.). Retrieved November 17, 2022, from https://www.businessinsider.in/sustainability/article/opinion-green-financing-in-india-need-significance-urgency-and-way-forward/ articleshow/92948265.cms

Sustainability Initiatives in the Financial Sector in India | Download Table. (n.d.). Retrieved November 17, 2022, from https://www.researchgate.net/ figure/Sustainability-Initiatives-in-the-Financial-Sector-in-India_tbl1_326738586

CHAPTER IV

Islamic Finance

Ms. Bhavi Desai; Parth Gohil; Surbhi Khuswah; Shruti Lathiya; Drishi Mehta

1. INTRODUCTION

Islamic finance is a financial system that follows Islamic law or Sharia. This economic system, like the traditional financial system, includes banks, insurance companies, investment firms, capital markets, and fund managers. In terms of rules, in addition to Islamic law, a few traditional financial system rules also apply to Islamic finance (Islamic Finance - Meaning, Principles, Concept, and More, 2022).

1. HISTORY

Islamic finance was virtually non-existent 30 years ago. Despite the fact that the industry is relatively new, Islamic economic theories have been around since the mid-12th century.(*Islamic Finance – Meaning, Principles, Concept and More,* 2022).

The origins of Islamic Finance

Islamic Finance is based on principles rooted in Islam and sourced from:
   - The Holy Quran
- The Sunnah (teachings, acts, or quotes of the Prophet Mohammad PBUH)
   While these are the primary sources for Islamic finance, to have a consensual approach and facilitate logical thinking, the following are also allowed:
   - Ijma (Consensus)
- Qiyas (Analogy)
- Ijtihad (Independent Reasoning) (*An Introduction to Islamic Finance and Its Impact on Trade - ICC Academy,* 2021).

3. CONCEPT

The concept of balance is central to the Islamic financial system. This concept emphasises that the system's goal should be to benefit society. Furthermore, the concept implies that Allah owns all wealth and that humans are merely trustees.

Humans must take care of this wealth in accordance with Allah's commands, promoting justice. Furthermore, Islamic economics implies that Muslims have the right to enjoy their wealth. They must spend it in accordance with Sharia law.

Islamic economics believes in a free-market economy governed by supply and demand rather than the government. It does, however, shape market functions by imposing a few rules and ethics. These laws and ethics contribute to social justice or balance.

To achieve social justice, Islamic finance employs the following strategies:

1. *Belief in Islam.*
2. *Taxing the wealthy and using the proceeds to assist those in need (zakat).*
3. *They are outlining the state's responsibilities.*
4. *They prohibit usury or interest.*
5. *Encourage group risk-taking (Islamic Finance – Meaning, Principles, Concept and More, 2022).*

4. PRINCIPLES OF ISLAMIC FINANCE

Islamic financial institutions adhere to a set of principles to ensure that they remain committed to their goals. These principles also distinguish Islamic institutions from other types of institutions. The principles are as follows:

- Interest Charges

The charging of interest is strictly forbidden in Islam. Interest is considered usury under Sharia law (riba). According to Islam, interest payments benefit lenders at the expense of borrowers. As a result, it forbids lenders and borrowers from charging or paying interest. Sharia-compliant banks do not make interest-based loans.

- There will be no investment in prohibited activities.

Some activities, such as dealing with alcohol or pork, are completely forbidden in Islam. These activities are prohibited by Islam (meaning forbidden). As a result, investing in such activities is prohibited by Islam.

- Speculation and gambling are prohibited (maisir)

Sharia prohibits all forms of speculation and gambling. As a result, Islamic financial institutions do not engage in any activity that is contingent on a future uncertain event.

- Uncertainty and danger (gharar)

Islam forbids engaging in activities involving excessive risk and uncertainty, such as derivative contracts and short-selling.

Apart from the prohibitions listed above, Islamic finance adheres to two additional principles:

- Transactional Importance

This means that every transaction conducted by Islamic financial institutions must be related to a genuine underlying economic transaction.

- Profit/Loss Split

According to Islamic economics, one party cannot benefit from a transaction more than the other. It means that parties in a transaction share the profit, loss, or risk.(*Islamic Finance – Meaning, Principles, Concept and More*, 2022).

5. INVESTMENT VEHICLES

Many traditional investment options in Islamic Finance, such as bonds, opportunities, and derivatives, are prohibited by Sharia. Thus, in Islamic Finance, there are primarily two types of investment options:

- Equities

Shares and private equity investments are permitted under Islamic finance. However, those businesses must not engage in activities that are prohibited by Islamic law, such as gambling, alcohol, pork, and interest-bearing lending.

- Fixed-income Instruments

There are no conventional bonds in the Islamic system because Sharia prohibits interest payments. Instead, they use Sukuk, also known as "Sharia-compliant bonds," which are not debt obligations but instead represent a portion of ownership.

- Insurance

Traditional insurance is prohibited under Islamic law because it involves dealing with an uncertain outcome. As a result, insurers employ a form of cooperative (mutual) insurance. Subscribers contribute money to a pool of funds, which the insurance company invests in accordance with Sharia principles. Companies pay claims from these funds, while policyholders split the profits.(An Introduction to Islamic Finance and Its Impact on Trade - ICC Academy, n.d.).

6. HOW DO ISLAMIC BANKS SURVIVE?

The question that naturally arises is, how do Islamic banks survive if they do not charge interest? Deposits are used to purchase assets by such banks. They then lease or resell (Ijara) the property for a higher price than the initial market value. The underlying idea is that instead of profiting from interest, these banks use customer funds to purchase assets.

Rather than making loans, these banks purchase assets on behalf of their customers. They then rent it to the same customer. The bank holds the title to the property. The customer acquires ownership of the property at the end of the lease period.

Furthermore, when investing in a business, Islamic banks do not charge interest. They instead opt for profit sharing. (Mudarabah) (*Islamic Finance – Meaning, Principles, Concept and More*, 2022).

7. ROLE OF ISLAMIC FINANCE IN INTERNATIONAL TRADE

Banks and financial institutions play an important role in international trade by bridging the gap between buyers and sellers of goods and services. Although it appears to be a simple process, moving a good or service from the seller (exporter) to the buyer (importer) involves many stakeholders, including customs, shipping companies, freight forwarders, warehousing agents, and so on.

All of these parties use various trade products such as letters of credit, documentary collections, open account trade, import loans, bill discounting, pre/post shipment finance, discounting, guarantees, and structured solutions such as receivables finance or supply chain finance, among others.

While Islamic banking alternatives to all conventional bank solutions are available, well established, and operationally similar, assigning responsibilities to different parties involved and sharing risk/return is a key differentiator for Islamic finance. This is in contrast to traditional finance, in which the financial institution serves primarily as a lender and bears no risk.

Example

Assume a customer in Dubai wishes to open a letter of credit (LC) in order to import machinery from China.

A traditional bank will open an LC for a commission for its client without taking any risk associated with the underlying goods. If a client requires additional financing for imported machinery, an import loan will be provided.

An Islamic Bank can provide 3 types of solutions based on different scenarios:

Wakalah LC - A loan in which the bank acts as the client's agent to import machinery for a fee. This is appropriate when a client does not require financing.

Murabaha LC - Where the bank acts as the owner of the machinery, assumes the risks associated with import, and sells the machinery to the client on the spot (if no financing is required), in instalments, or on deferred payment, depending on the client's needs. Alternatively, the bank can rent out machinery to the client (Ijarah) for a set period of time.

Musharakah LC - When the bank collaborates with the client to import machinery. This mode is appropriate if the client only requires partial financing. When the documents arrive, the bank can sell its share

to the client on the spot, in instalments, or on deferred payment, or it can give its part of ownership to the client on rent (Ijarah).

Everything an Islamic bank provides is also available through conventional financing. However, as demonstrated in this example, an Islamic bank is more than just a lender; rather, the relationship is based on risks and rewards.(*An Introduction to Islamic Finance and Its Impact on Trade - ICC Academy*, 2021).

8. TWO MAIN MODES OF ISLAMIC BANKING & FINANCE

- ISTISNA

Istisna is a long-term contractual agreement in Islamic finance for constructing, building, or manufacturing an asset, allowing for advance money payment and delivery of commodities at a predetermined future time at an agreed price. It is commonly used to provide a means of financing the construction or development of houses, buildings, plants, heavy machinery, and infrastructures such as roads, bridges, and railways.

- BAI SALAM

It is one of the most well-known methods of Islamic financing. Salam refers to an agreement in which advance payment is made for products that will be delivered later. The seller or dealer delivers some specific merchandise to the buyer at a later date in exchange for a development cost that is fully paid at the time of the agreement. It is critical that the nature of the product proposed for purchase be completely understood and determined, leaving no room for uncertainty, which can lead to conflict. This transaction involves a variety of goods that cannot include gold, silver, or currency. Nonetheless, Bai Salam covers nearly everything that can be measured in terms of quality, quantity, and craftsmanship, among other things.(*6 Major Modes Of Islamic Banking & Finance - Centre for Islamic Economic*, 2016).

9. THE FUTURE OF ISLAMIC FINANCE

Islamic finance is dynamic and ever-changing in response to the changing macroeconomic environment. With the upcoming challenges in a post-pandemic (COVID) world in mind, Islamic banks are changing their business practises through the use of technology.

For example, in certain modes such as Murabaha, Musharakah, Istisna, Ijarah, and Salam, where the bank acts as the owner of the goods, Islamic banks are required to physically inspect stocks. However, these were replaced with virtual visits to ensure SOPs were followed.

Similarly, banks are looking into blockchain solutions to reduce the need for physical interaction when submitting requests, documents, and sale contracts. In addition, the use of proprietary, dedicated online platforms is increasing.

Banks are also moving toward electronic document solutions, with an important component being the adoption of electronic bills of lading, which will represent a paradigm shift in the operations of key stakeholders such as shipping lines, customs, and banks.

Top Three Emerging Trends in Islamic Finance Due To COVID-19

1. **Accelerating Islamic finance's digitalization**
2. **Islamic social finance is being transformed.**
3. **Promoting sustainability and responsible investment**(*An Introduction to Islamic Finance and Its Impact on Trade - ICC Academy*, 2021).

10. ADVANTAGES OF ISLAMIC FINANCE

- Access to Islamic finance is not limited to Muslim communities, which may make it appealing to companies interested in ethical investing.
- Speculation is prohibited, lowering the risk of loss.
- Excessive profits are not permitted; only reasonable markups are permitted.
- Banks are less likely to fail because they cannot use excessive leverage.
- The rules encourage all parties to consider the long term, resulting in a more stable financial environment.
- Cooperation and profit generation through ethical and fair activity benefit the entire community.(*ACCA AFM Notes: B3b. Advantages of*

Islamic Finance | ACOWtancy Textbook, 2022).

11. DISADVANTAGES OF ISLAMIC FINANCE

- Sharia interpretations of new financial products are not always consistent. Some Murabaha are calculated based on current interest rates rather than economic or profit conditions.
- Documentation is frequently tailored to the transaction, resulting in high transaction/issue costs.
- Islamic finance institutions must comply with additional regulations, which raises issue/transaction costs.
- Banks must learn more than usual, necessitating additional due diligence.
- Because hedging is prohibited, Islamic banks cannot reduce their risks.
- Some Islamic products may violate international financial regulations.
- Sukuk product trading has been restricted, particularly since the financial crisis.
- With no interest, it is difficult to claim some Islamic instruments as debt, resulting in a loss of tax benefits and an increase in the WACC.(*ACCA AFM Notes: B3b. Disadvantages of Islamic Finance | ACOWtancy Textbook*, 2022).

Glossary

Ijarah – leasing of an asset by the owner to the tenant

Islamic – Governed by Shariah jurisprudence

Istisna – Sale of goods that currently do not exist and need manufacturing

Kafalah – A guarantee issued by a guarantor on behalf of the applicant

Mudarabah – Partnership where some partners contribute capital and others contribute services

Murabaha – Sale where the cost to the seller is disclosed to the buyer

Musawamah – Sale where the cost is not disclosed by the seller to the buyer

Musharakah – Partnership where all partners contribute capital

Riba – Gain (monetary or non-monetary) over and above the loan

Salam – Sale of homogeneous goods against 100% advance payment when goods don't currently exist.

Sale – exchange of one thing of value with another thing of value with mutual consent

Sukuk – Islamic bonds using Shariah-compliant underlying modes

Tawarruq – Also called commodity Murabaha, where a sale is used to generate capital, though the underlying goods are not required by the buyer

Wakalah – An agency arrangement where an agent provides services for a fee(*An Introduction to Islamic Finance and Its Impact on Trade - ICC Academy*, 2021).

References:

6 Major Modes Of Islamic Banking & Finance—Centre for Islamic Economic. (2016, April 9). http://cie.com.pk/6-major-modes-of-islamic-banking-finance/

ACCA AFM Notes: B3b. Advantages of Islamic finance | aCOWtancy Textbook. (2022, January 15). https://www.acowtancy.com/textbook/acca-afm/b3-impact-of-financing-on-investment-decisions-and-apv/advantages-of-islamic-finance/notes

ACCA AFM Notes: B3b. Disadvantages of Islamic finance | aCOWtancy Textbook. (2022, January 15). https://www.acowtancy.com/textbook/acca-afm/b3-impact-of-financing-on-investment-decisions-and-apv/disadvantages-of-islamic-finance/notes

An Introduction to Islamic Finance and its Impact on Trade—ICC Academy. (2021, August 21). https://icc.academy/islamic-finance-guide/

Islamic Finance – Meaning, Principles, Concept and More. (2022, June 23). https://efinancemanagement.com/sources-of-finance/islamic-finance

CHAPTER V

Crowd Funding

Ms. Anjali Denny; Ms. Samata Chaudhari; Ms. Saloni Chaudhary; Ms. Bhumi Patel

1.CROWDFUNDING

1.1 Introduction:

Crowdfunding is the use of small sums of money from a large number of people to fund a new business venture. Crowdfunding leverages the easy accessibility of vast networks of people via social media and crowdfunding websites to connect investors and entrepreneurs, with the potential to increase entrepreneurship by broadening the pool of investors beyond the traditional circle of owners, relatives, and venture capitalists.

Crowdfunding is a method of raising funds for a person or organisation by soliciting donations from family, friends, friends of friends, strangers, businesses, and others. People can reach more potential donors through social media than through traditional forms of fundraising. Crowdfunding is the use of small sums of money from a large number of people to fund a new business venture. Depending on the type of crowdfunding, investors can either donate money or receive rewards such as equity in the company that raised the funds.

The company is not required to repay investors in the case of donation-based crowdfunding. However, many companies provide early backers with perks such as an advance copy of the product. Crowdfunding has enabled entrepreneurs to raise hundreds of thousands or millions of dollars from anyone willing to invest. Crowdfunding allows anyone with an idea to pitch it in front of eager investors. One of the more amusing projects that received funding was from a person who wanted to develop a new potato salad recipe. His goal was to raise $10, but he ended up raising more than $55,000 from 6,911 backers. Investors can choose from hundreds of projects and put as little as $10 down. Crowdfunding websites make money by taking a percentage of the funds raised.

1.2 Market Overview:

Crowdfunding involves the exchange of a service or product for monetary contributions to a project or business. Crowdfunding is a popular fundraising method because it does not require any money to be returned.

Crowdfunding has become a popular way for many small businesses and creative projects to raise funds. It is used to raise funds for specific programmes such as R&D, the development of new prototypes, and the creation of new products. It enables direct market access without the need for venture capitalists or banks. It is considered a configurable, adaptable, and efficient fundraising solution when compared to traditional methods.

Last year, when global investors were flush with cash, they bet big on fledgling Indian companies, the Indian start-up storey received a lot of attention. In the third quarter of 2021, the number of deals and deal value were at an all-time high, and a slew of consumer-facing start-ups made spectacular debuts on the Indian stock exchange.

But if you thought this was the best of times for all Indian start-ups, think again. You'd be mistaken. For example, only about 7% of the 61,400 start-ups launched up to January 2022 were able to raise funds from PE or VC investors. The remaining 56,000 start-ups are still looking for ways to raise capital.

According to the data, Indian households' wealth and savings increased during the pandemic. Over the last two years, I've poured a lot of money into stocks, mutual funds, cryptocurrencies, and so on. Allowing retail investors with the means to take high risk a foothold in the start-up ecosystem via the crowdfunding channel may be a good idea. Not only will this allow small investors to benefit from the vibrant start-up ecosystem, it will also provide a more sustainable source of funds for the upcoming companies.

Community crowdfunding platforms are legal and permitted to operate in India. The RBI regulates peer-to peer lending activities, one of the two types of financial returns crowdfunding. However, SEBI has yet to develop regulations for equity crowdfunding, which can be used by early-stage start-ups to raise capital.

2. CONCEPTUAL FRAMEWORK

2.1 Types of Crowdfunding:

The two most traditional uses of the term reflect the type of crowdfunding done by start-up companies looking to bring a product or service into the world, as well as by individuals who have experienced an emergency. Many people who have been affected by a natural disaster, a large medical bill, or another tragic event such as a house fire have received financial assistance that they would not have received otherwise thanks to crowdfunding platforms. In recent years, however, some crowdfunding platforms, such as Patreon and Sub stack, have expanded the reach of crowdfunding to provide a way for creative people—artists, writers, musicians, or podcasters—to sustain their creative work by receiving a steady source of income.

While there are four types of crowdfunding, each one receives funds from willing donors. Here's a rundown of each:

- ***Donation-Based Crowdfunding***

- Disaster relief
- Charities
- Non-profits
- Medical bills
- Product development

Have you ever donated to a worthy cause? Or in support of an innovative idea that has piqued your interest? You probably donated to a donation-based crowdfunding campaign. Donations are typically made in small amounts by supporters with the expectation that they will receive no incentives in return.

- ***Rewards-Based Crowdfunding***

- Individuals contributing gain a 'reward' (e.g. a form of a product or service a company offers)
- Companies can increase contributors but without losing ownership
- Generally used for start-ups
- Anyone can contribute
- Companies tend to offer pre-orders and custom incentives
- Typically raising less than $50,000

Individuals who contribute to this type of crowdfunding are rewarded. This is a great way to say thank you to your investors without breaking the bank. It's a win-win situation for everyone.

- ***Equity-Based Crowdfunding:*** - Contributors become part-owners of the company

- Trading capital for equity shares
- Financial return for investment
- Receive share of the profits in the form of dividend or distribution
- Typically raising $50,000 to $10 million
- Done through registered portals that must meet certain criteria
- This is one of the riskiest methods of crowdfunding, but it allows investors to enter private equity markets and diversify their portfolios. The United States changed its regulations in 2015, allowing anyone to invest in a campaign with certain restrictions.

- *Debt-Based Crowdfunding:*

    - Investors lend money with a promise of their money being returned with interest

  - Investor submit amount they want to invest and interest of return
  - Once filled, final rate of return is calculated using an average of all bids submitted
  - No banks involved
  - Loans agreed faster
  - Generally requires:
  - Good credit history
  - Solid Financials
  - Debt-based crowdfunding allows a group of people to lend funds to individuals and businesses. After which, investors would gain interest with steady repayments with low interest. This form of crowdfunding is best for companies that have assets and cash flow to service the loans. Risks are significantly less in comparison to equity-based crowdfunding.

3. ADVANTAGES AND DISADVANTAGES

- **Advantages:**

- It can be a quick way to raise funds with no upfront costs.
- Pitching a project or business online can be a valuable form of marketing and can result in media attention.

- When you share your idea, you can frequently receive feedback and expert advice on how to improve it.
- It is a good way to test the public's reaction to your product/idea - if people are eager to invest, it is a good sign that your idea has a good chance of succeeding in the market. Investors can track your progress - this may help you promote your brand through their networks.

- **Disadvantages:**

- When you are on your chosen platform, you must do a lot of work to generate interest before launching the project - significant resources (money and/or time) may be required.
- If you fail to meet your funding goal, any funds pledged will usually be returned to your investors, and you will receive nothing.
- Failed projects endanger your company's reputation and the people who have pledged money to you.
- Someone may see your business idea on a crowdfunding site and steal it if you haven't protected it with a patent or copyright.
- Getting the rewards or returns wrong can result in investors receiving too much of the business.

- **Benefits for the Creator Edit**

- Crowdfunding campaigns provide producers with several advantages in addition to financial gains. The following are some of the non-monetary benefits of crowdfunding.
- A compelling project can raise a producer's profile and improve their reputation.
- Marketing - project initiators can demonstrate that their project has an audience and a market. In the event of a failed campaign, it provides useful market feedback. It also has a signal value: observing consumers, including those who were not involved in the original crowdfunding campaign, show a strong preference for crowdfunded products over those funded through alternative means.
- Crowdfunding provides a forum for project initiators to interact with their target audiences. An audience can participate in the production process by following updates from the creators and providing feedback through comment features on the project's crowdfunding page.

- Feedback - Giving project backers pre-release access to content or the opportunity to beta-test content as part of the funding incentives provides the project initiators with immediate access to good market testing feedback.

- **Risks and Barriers for the Creator Edit**

While crowdfunding is gaining popularity, it also has a number of potential risks or barriers. According to studies, crowdfunding contains "high levels of risk, uncertainty, and information asymmetry" for both the creator and the investor.

- *Reputation* – Failure to meet campaign objectives or generate interest leads to public failure. Reaching financial targets and garnering significant public support, but failing to deliver on a project for whatever reason, can have a significant negative impact on one's reputation.

- *Intellectual property (IP) protection* – Because of concerns about idea theft and protecting their intellectual property (IP) from plagiarism, many Interactive Digital Media developers and content producers are hesitant to publicly announce the details of a project before production. Creators who use crowdfunding must release their product to the public during the early stages of funding and development, exposing themselves to the risk of competitor copying.

- *Donor exhaustion* – There is a risk that contacting the same network of supporters multiple times will cause that network to stop providing necessary support.
- *Public fear of abuse* – Supporters are concerned that without a regulatory framework, the likelihood of a scam or misuse of funds is high. The fear may become a barrier to public participation.
- *Lack of participation* – Based on the story, some stories are more likely to be picked up than others. If you "just tell a story," it is simple to gain support.

4. APPLICATIONS OF CROWDFUNDING:
Crowdfunding can be used for a wide range of projects, which is why it is used in so many industries, including education, healthcare, and arts and

culture. There are no hard and fast rules that say something can or cannot be crowdfunded. The success of the idea or project will be determined by the crowd.

Colleges and Universities

Did you participate in a team or club while at university or college? You may be aware of the scarcity of funds for many extracurricular activities. This is why student organisations have turned to crowdfunding. The same issue can afflict research projects as well as social causes. Crowdfunding projects are a simple, low-cost way to improve existing departments or organisations.

Moreover, unlike traditional fundraising activities, crowdfunding allows you to broaden the reach of your campaign, promote the good work being done on campus, and raise far more money in a much shorter period of time.

Crowdfunding is well-known on college campuses across North America. So much so that Suffolk University's Sawyer Business School in Boston offers a course on the importance of crowdfunding to students. Students in the course manage their own Crowdfunding campaigns.

Healthcare

The healthcare industry is home to some of the most cutting-edge research and product development. There are projects that aim to improve communication between healthcare providers and their patients; there are products that provide people with information on how to live a healthy lifestyle; and there are projects that aim to bring new treatments to market and improve patient outcomes.

These kinds of projects are ideal for crowdsourcing. Everyone is affected by health issues in some way, and a successful crowdfunding campaign will put your project in front of people who want to support medical, healthy living, and patient care innovations.

Cure Crowd is a medically guided search engine that helps users find genuine medical evaluations and answers. It takes more than just Googling symptoms to find possible ailments on WebMD. It's a more effective way of researching your personal health concerns. This was a company that used crowdfunding to get their project off the ground.

Eve Medical is another successful crowdfunding success story. Throughout medical history, research and treatment have not always been focused on the specific health needs of women. Eve Medical is committed to creating innovative, user-centered medical products for women.

Culture and the Arts

Arts and culture are popular crowdfunding categories. Whether you need funding to produce a film or record an album, or to support a theatre or art installation, crowdfunding can be a powerful tool for getting your project in front of patrons who want to support the arts.

Virtual Choir, a crowdfunding project, was launched in August of 2013. The goal was to bring together individual singers from all over the world. Singers sent in their own tapes, which were later edited to be played simultaneously, creating a choir-like experience. A video of art and sketches sent by others was also included in the performance.artists.

5. RECENT TRENDS IN CROWDFUNDING

During the forecast period, the crowdfunding market is expected to grow at a CAGR of more than 16 percent (2021-2026). Crowdfunding is the practise of soliciting small sums of money from an undefined group of people known as the crowd. Crowdfunding platforms could act as go-betweens for donors and recipients. This intermediary could use a variety of marketing techniques to influence the potential donor's behaviour. As a result, it is critical to look for the influencing factors that are used to raise funds on crowdfunding platforms such as social media platforms.

Furthermore, according to Fundly, the global amount raised by crowdfunding in 2019 was in the thirties of USD billion. Furthermore, it is estimated that 6,445,080 crowdfunding campaigns were held globally in 2019. Furthermore, by 2025, the crowdfunding market is expected to triple.

Social media platforms serve as free promotion resources for crowdfunding organisations seeking a global audience reach. It has made it easier for businesses to conduct product pre-selling and marketing. As a result, active crowdfunding campaigns on social media are expected to fuel the growth of the crowdfunding market in the coming years. According to startups.com, 12% of Facebook shares, 3% of Twitter shares, and 53% of email shares convert to donations.

The gaming industry company is witnessing the most successful fundraising campaign to raise funds. Technology campaigns can also attract crowdfunding. According to the Kickstarter crowdfunding platform, it raised over USD 1 million, with gaming campaigns accounting for 37% of successful campaigns and technology campaigns accounting for 30% of successful campaigns.

Many companies, including Kickstarter PBC, Indiegogo Inc., GoFundMe Inc., Crowdfunder Inc., and Alibaba Group, provide a crowdfunding platform to raise funds for various initiatives. In October 2019, the crowdsourcing platform Kickstarter received over USD 4.5 billion in pledges for various projects.

With the recent COVID-19 outbreak, the crowdfunding market is experiencing significant growth, particularly donation crowdfunding to support and help communities, people, and many organisations fight this pandemic. For example, in April 2020, Facebook launched "Facebook Fundraiser," a platform where people can raise money for charity to aid others in the event of a pandemic.

In April 2020, various crowdfunding platforms in India raised more than INR 100 crore to help people in need. During the pandemic, these online crowdfunding campaigns assist stranded migrants, daily wage labourers, transgender communities, circus performers, Uber drivers, Swiggy delivery personnel, rural artisans, dancers, and freelance workers.

Chart 1: Global crowdfunding market

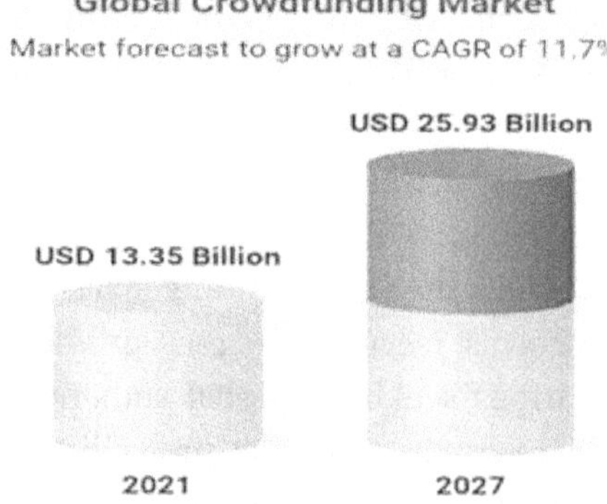

(source: https://www.globenewswire.com/en/news-release/2022/04/08/2419116/28124/en/global-crowdfunding-market-2022-to-2027-industry-trends-share-size-growth-opportunity-and-forecasts.html)

6. CHALLENGES OF CROWDFUNDING

Product/Project Replication: This is possible because there are a large number of participants, and an idea or concept can be stolen by someone else because the owner does not have the exclusive right to make, use, or sell the invention in a pattern period of time due to the nature of the crowdfunding projects.

Inadequate communication: Lack of tangible objectives and indistinguishable goals can make it difficult for potential stockholders to determine how true the entrepreneurs' expectations are. Unrealistic financial goals that project carriers occasionally request that are excessive or insufficient. If they ask for too much, potential shareholders may think they are materialistic, and if they ask for too little, shareholders may question whether the project carriers understand what they are doing.

Slow updating: People do not donate money to crowdfunding concepts, but they are willing to donate their time and attention. It is critical to encourage sponsors to return frequently. Failure to post updates throughout the technique may result in the loss of potential shareholders. There is no clear budget. The entrepreneur has no idea how to spend the money he has collected in an efficient manner. The project details show potential sponsors where their money is going, and budget sharing is the first stepping stone that separates the projects that just look interesting from the projects that actually have a logical chance of producing the expected results.

Creativity: It is the key to launching a successful movement. In this economy, whoever can attract, drag, or pull the crowd's attention will win. According to the crowd-funding platforms, the more creatively presented projects have a higher success rate.

Complex Business Concept: Crowdfunding entrepreneur may not be appropriate for the complex business concept that people may find difficult to comprehend. If they want to invite investors on a crowdfunding website, they must be able to explain their business idea in a well-defined manner that is clear, short, and charming.

References:

Crowdfunding, https://www.crowdfunding.com/. Accessed 19 November 2022..

https://www.investopedia.com/terms/c/crowdfunding.asp. Accessed 19 November 2022.

://www.crowdfunding.com/

Smith, Tim. "Crowdfunding: What It Is, How It Works, Popular Websites." *Investopedia,* https://www.investopedia.com/terms/c/crowdfunding.asp. Accessed 19 November 2022.

Smith, Tim. "Crowdfunding: What It Is, How It Works, Popular Websites." *Investopedia,*

The Basics of Crowdfunding for Your Business - businessnewsdaily.com. (n.d.). Business News Daily. Retrieved November 20, 2022, from https://www.businessnewsdaily.com/4134-what-is-crowdfunding.html

10 Pros and Cons of Business Crowdfunding. (2022, March 29). Fit Small Business. Retrieved November 20, 2022, from https://fitsmallbusiness.com/pros-cons-business-crowdfunding/

Gillman, M. (2022, March 15). *The advantages of crowdfunding.* Bake Magazine. Retrieved November 20, 2022, from https://www.bakemag.com/articles/15845-the-advantages-of-crowdfunding

Carolla, A. (n.d.). *List of highest-funded crowdfunding projects.* Wikipedia. Retrieved November 20, 2022, from https://en.m.wikipedia.org/wiki/List_of_highest-funded_crowdfunding_projects

Crowdfunding for Startups: Kickstarter Alternatives - businessnewsdaily.com. (2022, June 29). Business News Daily. Retrieved November 20, 2022, from https://www.businessnewsdaily.com/4847-crowdfunding-small-business.html

https://www.businessnewsdaily.com/4847-crowdfunding-small-business.html (*Crowdfunding for Startups: Kickstarter Alternatives - Businessnewsdaily.com,* 2022)

Smith, T. (n.d.). *Crowdfunding: What It Is, How It Works, Popular Websites.* Investopedia. Retrieved November 20, 2022, from https://www.investopedia.com/terms/c/crowdfunding.asp

Fronea, C. (n.d.). *History of crowdfunding.* Smallbrooks. Retrieved November 20, 2022, from https://smallbrooks.com/history-of-crowdfunding/

Banking - Crowdfunding in India. (n.d.). IndiaFilings. Retrieved November 20, 2022, from https://www.indiafilings.com/learn/crowdfunding-in-india/

Francom, S. R. (n.d.). *Best Crowdfunding Sites for Startups in 2022.* Business.org. Retrieved November 20, 2022, from https://www.business.org/finance/loans/best-crowdfunding-sites-for-startups/

How about crowdfunding for start-ups? - The Hindu BusinessLine. (2022, July 7). The Hindu Business Line. Retrieved November 20, 2022, from https://www.thehindubusinessline.com/opinion/how-about-crowdfunding-for-start-ups/article65608857.ece

Global Crowdfunding Market (2022 to 2027) - Industry Trends, Share, Size, Growth, Opportunity and Forecasts. (2022, April 8). Send Press Releases with GlobeNewswire. Retrieved November 20, 2022, from https://www.globenewswire.com/en/news-release/2022/04/08/2419116/28124/en/Global-Crowdfunding-Market-2022-to-2027-Industry-Trends-Share-Size-Growth-Opportunity-and-Forecasts.html

Introduction to Crowdfunding. (2017, May 30). Make Giving Happen. Retrieved November 20, 2022, from https://makegivinghappen.com/introduction-to-crowdfunding/

CHAPTER VI

BASEL Accord for Banks

Ms. Chitra Jethva; Ms. Rinkal Lad; Ms. Khushboo Khambhati; Ms. Axita Chodvadiya; Mr. Jayesh Joshi

1. INTRODUCTION

1.1 What are Basel norms?

The Basel Committee on Banking Supervision issues international banking regulations known as Basel norms or Basel accords.

The Basel norms are an international effort to coordinate banking regulations with the goal of strengthening the international banking system.

It is the collection of Basel Committee on Banking Supervision agreements that focuses on the risks to banks and the financial system.

1.2 Why the name Basel?

Basel is a city located in Switzerland. It is the headquarters of the Bureau of International Settlements (BIS), which promotes cooperation among central banks in the pursuit of financial stability and common banking regulatory standards. It was established in 1930. The Basel Committee on Banking Supervision is headquartered in Basel, Switzerland.

1.3 Why these norms?

Banks lend to various types of borrowers, each with their own set of risks. They lend public deposits as well as money raised in the market, i.e. equity and debt. This exposes the bank to a variety of default risks, and as a result, they occasionally fall. As a result, banks must set aside a certain percentage of capital as collateral against the risk of non-recovery. To address this risk, the Basel committee developed Basel Norms for Banking.

1.4 What are these norms?

The Basel Committee has issued three sets of regulations which are known as Basel-I, II, and III.

Basel-I

It first appeared in 1988. It was almost entirely concerned with credit risk. The possibility of a loss due to a borrower's failure to repay a loan or meet contractual obligations is referred to as credit risk. It traditionally refers to the risk that a lender will not receive the principal and interest owed. It established the capital and risk-weighting structure for banks. The required minimum capital was set at 8% of risk-weighted assets (RWA). RWA refers to assets with varying risk profiles. For example, an asset backed by collateral would be less risky than a personal loan with no collateral. In 1999, India adopted the Basel-I guidelines.

Basel-II

1. BCBS published Basel II guidelines in 2004. These were the improved and reformed versions of the Basel I agreement. The guidelines were founded on three pillars, as the committee refers to them.
2. Capital Adequacy Standards: Banks should keep a minimum capital adequacy requirement of 8% of risk assets.
3. Supervisory Review: According to this, banks were required to develop and implement better risk management techniques in order to monitor and manage all three types of risks that a bank faces, namely credit, market, and operational risks.
4. Market Discipline: Increased disclosure requirements are required. Banks must disclose their CAR, risk exposure, and other information to the central bank.
5. Basel II norms have yet to be fully implemented in India and elsewhere, despite the fact that India abides by them.

Basel III

Basel III guidelines were published in 2010. These guidelines were put in place in response to the 2008 financial crisis. The system needed to be strengthened further because banks in developed economies were undercapitalized, over-leveraged, and relied more on short-term funding. It was also felt that the amount and quality of capital required under Basel II were insufficient to contain any additional risk. The guidelines seek to promote a more resilient banking system by concentrating on four critical banking parameters: capital, leverage, funding, and liquidity.

- Capital: The capital adequacy ratio should be kept at 12.9 percent. The minimum Tier 1 and Tier 2 capital ratios must be maintained at 10.5 percent and 2 percent of risk-weighted assets, respectively. Furthermore, banks must maintain a **capital conservation buffer** of 2.5 percent. The counter-cyclical buffer should also be kept at 0-2.5 percent.
- Leverage: The leverage rate must be at least 3%. The leverage rate is the ratio of a bank's tier 1 capital to total consolidated assets on average.

- Liquidity and funding: Basel-III established two liquidity ratios: the LCR and the NSFR.
- The liquidity coverage ratio: LCR will require banks to keep a buffer of high-quality liquid assets sufficient to cover cash outflows in an acute short-term stress scenario as specified by supervisors. This is to prevent situations like "Bank Run". The goal is to ensure that banks have enough liquidity to survive a 30-day stress scenario.
- The Net Stable Funds Rate: NSFR mandates that banks maintain a consistent funding profile in relation to their off-balance-sheet assets and activities. The NSFR requires banks to fund their operations with stable sources of funding (reliable over the one-year horizon). The NSFR must be at least 100 percent. LCR thus measures short-term (30-day) resilience, whereas NSFR measures medium-term (1-year) resilience.

In India, the deadline for implementing Basel-III was March 2019. It was pushed back to March 2020. Because of the coronavirus pandemic, the RBI decided to postpone the implementation of Basel standards for another 6 months.

Extending the time period under Basel III results in a lower capital burden on banks in terms of provisioning requirements, including NPAs.

This extension would have an impact on how Indian banks and central banks are perceived by global players.

1.5 The Basel committee on banking supervision

The Basel Committee on Banking Supervision (BCBS) is the primary global standard setter for bank prudential regulation and serves as a forum for regular cooperation on banking supervisory matters among central banks around the world.

It was founded in 1974 by the Central Bank Governors of the Group of Ten countries. The committee's membership was expanded in 2009 and again in 2014. The BCBS now has 45 members from 28 jurisdictions, including Central Banks and banking regulatory authorities.

It serves as a forum for regular collaboration on banking supervision issues. Its goal is to improve understanding of key supervisory issues and the quality of banking supervision globally.

2. ADVANTAGES AND DISADVANTAGES

2.1 Basel I

Advantages:

- Capital Adequacy has increased significantly. Bank ratios with international operations.
- Internationally active banks must compete on an equal footing.
- Capital management is improved.
- A financial evaluation standard for users of financial information.

Disadvantages:

- Other types of risk, such as market risk, operational risk, liquidity risk, and so on, were not taken into account.
- The book values of assets are prioritised over market values.

2.2 Basel II
Advantages:

- Because of the strict capital requirement norms, it has made the banking sector more secure.
- Strict supervision has assisted many banks in adhering to the minimum capital requirement. This practise has assisted banks in avoiding the worst-case scenario.

Disadvantage:

- The importance of the critical capital ratios that help predict the shortfall was lacking.
- The minimum capital requirements were not established with extreme outcomes in mind. In a severe crisis, even Basel II regulations cannot save a bank. If a bank has overinvested in risky assets and the market as a whole falls, the capital reserve will be useless. A bank run is imminent.

2.3 Basel III
Advantages:

- Greatly reduce the severity of economic downturns as well as the likelihood of future banking crises..

Disadvantage:

- Borrowers have increased their financial risks by concentrating sales in fewer segments and investing more in intangible assets, R&D, and capital expenditures, resulting in greater volatility in performance and the risk of default.

3. CURRENT SITUATION
3.1 Impact on Indian Banking System

- Systematic risk has been reduced, and economic and financial stress has been absorbed.
- Weaker banks face a survival challenge.
- Institutional reorganisation through more mergers and acquisitions.
- Increased chances of international arbitration.

The Indian banking system has largely escaped the global financial crisis unscathed. This is due, among other things, to the relatively strong capitalization of Indian banks. The Reserve Bank of India (RBI) has set April 2013 as the start date for implementing Basel III norms over a 6-year period.

The recent requirement for additional equity infusion in light of low economic growth and rising non-performing assets in Indian banks paints a bleak picture.

Table 1: Comparison of Basel 2, 2.5 and 3

	Basel II	**Basel 2.5**	**Basel III**
Date of Issue	2004 Implemented in EU under CRD 2006	2011	2010 (proposed) 2013-2019 (implementation period)
Purpose	"three pillars" concept was introduced More risk sensitive	Adds market risk capital requirements	Created in respect to the global financial crisis
The main area of focus	"three pillars" concept was introduced: I. Minimum capital requirements II. Supervisory review III. Market discipline	Stressed value at risk A new trading book framework with an increased Risk Capital Charge (IRC) A new measure to correlate trading activities – Comprehensive Risk Measures (CRM)	Credit Risk Market Risk Operational Risk Liquidity Risk +2 new liquidity ratio: • Liquidity Coverage Ratio • Net Stable Funding Ratio
CAR- Capital Adequacy Ratio	The total capital ratio must be no lower than 8% Tier 2 capital is limited to 100% of Tier 1 capital	------------	CET 1.2%-> 4% Capital Conservation buffer 2.5%-> 7% Counter cyclical Buffer between 0% - 2.5% Leverage Ratio – 3% ow funds

(*Google Image Result*, n.d.)

The phased implementation of Basel III norms began in India on April 1, 2013, with full compliance initially targeted for March 31, 2018, but extended to March 31, 2019. The Indian banking system faces the challenge of meeting the stringent requirements of the Basel III framework while maintaining growth and profitability. The RBI sets a minimum Capital to Risk Weighted Asset Ratio (CRAR) of 9 percent, which is higher than the Basel III agreement's 8 percent requirement. Even though Indian banks appear to be well capitalised at 13 percent CRAR, they face enormous challenges in adopting Basel III.

Banks will face increased capital requirements as credit requirements for financing growth rise. There will also be a fiscal burden if the Indian government retains a majority shareholding.

To comply with the Basel III norms, Indian banks must raise a significant amount of capital over the next five years.

According to the CARE, the total equity capital requirement for Indian banks until March 2019 (when Basel III will be fully implemented) is likely to be in the range of Rs.1.5-1.8 trillion, assuming average GDP growth of 6% and average credit growth of 15% to 16% over the next five years. Again, it is estimated that the bank will earn a return on total assets of 0.6 percent and will meet the minimum regulatory requirement of CAR.

India is working to put in place a capital framework that mandates margin requirements for non-centrally cleared derivatives. This is interpreted as a push for central clearing.

An Expert Committee to Revise and Strengthen the Monetary Policy Framework recommended in January 2014 that the SLR be reduced to be consistent with the Liquidity Coverage Ratio, as required by the Basel III framework. This recommendation aims to improve monetary policy transmission in India.

In addition to the Basel III framework, the RBI intends to use its new Risk Based Supervision (RBS) framework, which includes an internal Supervisory Program for Risk and Capital (SPARC) and regular stress tests.

SIFIs (Systematically Important Financial Institutions) will be regulated, supervised, and scrutinised. Prior to the implementation of Basel III, the Indian banking system had a systemic Return on Equity of 13%. However, the same was significantly lower in the RBI stress test. This emphasised the significance of strengthening the Indian banking system.

In February 2012, the RBI issued draught regulations on liquidity risk management (LRM). Following the incorporation of comments and feedback, the final regulation was issued in November 2012. The regulation then stated that the final rules based on Basel III liquidity standards, namely Basel III: The Liquidity Coverage Ratio and Liquidity Risk Monitoring Tools (January 2013), will be issued once the Basel Committee has finalised the same.

One of the primary goals of banking sector reforms in the 1990s was to improve bank profitability and operational efficiency. Over this time period, the Cost to Income ratio (CI), Net Interest Margin (NIM), and Return on Assets (ROA) all show a decline in Cl and NIM for the entire banking system, but an improvement in ROA. According to Basel II standards, banks should aim for a Cl of 40% and a ROA of more than 1%.

India's performance in these two benchmarks compares favourably in the decade beginning in 2000, indicating an improvement in the efficiency of the Indian banking sector in recent years. The government is deeply concerned about public sector banks' declining capital adequacy, given the fiscal implications of additional capital infusion. While public sector banks meet the statutory CRAR target, the quality and quantity of (common equity) will need to be improved as they transition to Basel III standards (Nisha, n.d., Basel Norms and Their Impact on the Indian Banking System)

6. CONCLUSION AND FUTURE PERSPECTIVE

At some level, the Basel norms seek to create a fairly homogeneous global banking system. While this goal purports to strengthen the financial system, it may actually be its undoing. In other words, a homogeneous banking system may be more vulnerable to widespread failure or collapse.

Simply put, a diverse group is advantageous because an attack only affects a small percentage of its constituents. A banking system that is too homogeneous is actually dangerous for the future of countries all over the world.

References:

Basel Norms. (n.d.). Retrieved November 20, 2022, from https://www.drishtiias.com/to-the-points/paper3/basel-norms

Basel norms & impact on indian banking system nisha. (n.d.). Retrieved November 28, 2022, from https://www.slideshare.net/nishakapadia/basel-norms-impact-on-indian-banking-system-nisha

Google Image Result. (n.d.). Retrieved November 28, 2022, from https://www.google.com/imgres?imgurl=https://abhipedia.abhimanu.com/userfiles/basel(1).jpg&imgrefurl=https://abhipedia.abhimanu.com/Article/IAS/NDI2OAEEQQVVEEQQVV/Basel-Norms-and-Banking-System-of-India-a-critical-anaysis-Economic-Affairs&tbnid=cVflgbPcNu4Q5M&vet=1&docid=T-H66sLLC0R9hM&w=700&h=450&source=sh/x/im

(PDF) Basel III norms and Indian banks—a new definition of risk management. (n.d.). Retrieved November 20, 2022, from https://www.researchgate.net/publication/335685398_Basel_III_norms_and_Indian_banks-a_new_definition_of_risk_management

(PDF) Shift from Basel II to Basel III — A reporting perspective on the Indian banking sector. (n.d.). Retrieved November 20, 2022, from https://www.researchgate.net/publication/283302507_Shift_from_Basel_II_to_Basel_III_-_A_reporting_perspective_on_the_Indian_banking_sector

Reserve Bank of India—Publications. (n.d.). Retrieved November 20, 2022, from https://m.rbi.org.in//Scripts/PublicationsView.aspx?id=20990

62

CHAPTER VII

Reverse Mortgage Products for the Indian Market

Mr. Nikunj Khunt; Mr. Jay Italiya; Mr. Yash Jain

1. INTRODUCTION:

The global market for Old Age Social and Income Security (OASIS) products are Projected to grow substantially and India is no exception. Defined benefit schemes, both publicly and privately funded, are facing many risks and their viability is under threat. This has prompted the development of many products for sharing such risks, with pure defined contribution plans at one extreme. In fact, the Government of India (GOI) has shifted all its recent recruits to such a defined contribution plan. However, defined Contribution plans convert only the financial savings during working age into income Streams in old age.

To the extent savings during working age is locked up in house property, it cannot be encashed for old age needs except through selling and / or moving out. This would be the Case even if traditional loans were taken against house property, as they have to be Repaid, either through instalments or on maturity. This is where reverse mortgage (RM) Has a potential market: as an instrument to convert equity in a house property into an Income stream, without any debt servicing or relocating worries. RM products are not Available in India as of now. This paper is based on a small desk research and contains the following:

• A Survey of Literature on RM, both academic as well as practice oriented

• Preliminary exploration of India specific issuesThe global market for Old Age Social and Income Security (OASIS) products is expected to expand significantly, with India being no exception. Defined benefit schemes, both publicly and privately funded, face numerous risks, and their viability is jeopardised. As a result, many products for sharing such risks have been developed, with pure defined contribution plans at one extreme. Indeed, the Government of India (GOI) has moved all of its recent hires to a defined contribution plan. However, defined contribution plans only convert financial savings made during working years into income streams in retirement.

Savings made during working years are locked up in house property and cannot be cashed out for old age needs unless sold and/or moved out. This would be true even if traditional loans were taken out against real estate, as they must be repaid, either in instalments or at maturity. This is where reverse mortgages (RM) have a potential market: as a tool for converting equity in a home into an income stream with no debt servicing or relocating concerns. RM products are not currently available in India.

2. HOME EQUITY CONVERSION PRODUCTS :

RM is only one of several actual or potential financial instruments that could allow a homeowner to obtain liquid funds against his home equity. Tightly integrated housing markets, housing finance, including secondary markets, and home equity conversion can all improve social welfare in a variety of ways [2, 3, 4]. Home equity conversion products may be useful to anyone who is "house-rich but cash-poor," not just the elderly.

2.1 The range of such home equity conversion products includes the following :

- Reverse Mortgage
- Home Reversion / Sale and Lease Back

The homeowner sells his house outright but keeps the right to live in it for the rest of his life for a nominal/reduced rent. The proceeds of the sale may be paid in a lump sum or as an annuity. This might be an intra-family transaction.

- Interest-only Mortgage

This could be useful for those who require an immediate lump sum but have limited loan-servicing capacity. The borrower is only required to make interest payments during the Loan's term. The principal is only due upon maturity, death, permanent relocation, or sale.

- Mortgage Annuity/ Home Income

This is appropriate for the elderly, for whom life annuity rates are more appealing. The loan proceeds are used to purchase a life annuity. The annuity is deducted for mortgage interest, and the balance is paid as periodic income. The principal is repaid when the owner dies or the house is sold. The appeal is that the annuity will continue even if the borrower sells the house or permanently relocates.

- Shared Appreciation Mortgage

This provides loans at interest rates lower than the market. The loan is repaid upon death, relocation, or sale. In exchange, the lender receives a pre-agreed-upon share of any increase in property value over the loan's accumulated value.

As the RM market in the United States grew, some of these features were incorporated as options in the standard RM product. As a result, the distinctions made above are not Watertight.

3. REVERSE MORTGAGE – THE CONCEPT:

RM is essentially the inverse of a conventional mortgage loan.

A conventional mortgage loan begins with a large loan and little equity in the borrower's home. As he makes regular mortgage payments, he reduces his outstanding loan balance and builds his home equity.

In contrast, an RM borrower begins with a large amount of equity in his home. The lender makes a non-recourse loan secured by the house. The borrower has the option of receiving the proceeds through

- A lump sum at the start
- Monthly payments for a fixed term or a life-long annuity
- Establishing a credit line with or without interest accrual on credit balance

- A combination of the foregoing

The borrower is not required to leave the house or make any payments to the lender as long as he is alive and continues to live in it or does not sell it. As a result, the loan and interest accumulate until maturity. Satisfied has no credit or income requirements. Even if the total loan and interest exceeds the realisable value of the house at disposal, the repayment is limited to that amount only. As a result, RM is a case of 'increasing debt, decreasing equity'.

Understandably, the loan amount will be determined by

- The borrower's and any co-age applicant's (life expectancy/mortality risks)
- The current value of the property and the expected rate of appreciation (real Estate market risk)
- The current interest rate and the volatility of interest rates (interest rate risk)
- Closure and maintenance costs
- Specific features selected: Fixed or floating interest; appreciation shared; interest Earning credit-line; and, if applicable, mortgage insuranceThe borrower's and any co-age applicant's (life expectancy/mortality risks)
- The current value of the property and the expected rate of appreciation (real Estate market risk)
- The current interest rate and the volatility of interest rates (interest rate risk)
- Closure and maintenance costs
- Specific features selected: Fixed or floating interest; appreciation shared; interest Earning credit-line; and, if applicable, mortgage insurance

There is nothing in the reverse mortgage concept that limits it to the elderly. However, the product is especially suited for the elderly: in fact, the older a person is, the more appealing RM is. The reasons for the same are:

RM necessitates near total equity ownership of the home, which is more likely for people over the age of 50. (unless the property is inherited)

It is only appealing to people with insufficient current income and little financial savings—in other words, retirees.

The higher the additional income through an RM for a given property value, the lower the life expectancy (older the person is).

If the borrowers are elderly, public policy support, including tax breaks, is more likely.

The elderly are especially likely to place a high psychological/emotional/sentimental value on "ageing in place" without moving out. In fact, given the benefits of a familiar neighbourhood, the longer they have lived in their current home, the more valuable it is likely to be.

European investors purchased homes from elderly people 400 years ago and allowed them to live in the same house rent-free for the rest of their lives. During the 1929 crash, the concept of home-reversion was developed in the United Kingdom. In France, similar arrangements known as "visages" were available. The concept was later introduced to the United States, where it has grown and evolved the most in terms of variety and volume.

4. CURRENT VOLUMES IN THE U.S RM MARKETS:

According to http://www.reversemortgage.org, the website of The National Reverse Mortgage Lenders Association (NRMLA) of the United States, the current volumes and projections for the US market are as follows:

More than 80,000 reverse mortgages have been originated in the United States to date...

During the most recent federal fiscal year, which ended September 30, 2002, lenders closed a record 13,049 Home Equity Conversion Mortgage [HECM] Loans, a 63 percent increase over the previous record of 7,982 set in FY 1999.

The volume figure for this year (FY 2002) was 68 percent higher than the 7,781 HECMs closed in FY 2001.

Between 1989 and 1999, approximately $1 billion in reverse mortgage loan proceeds were advanced. Between 1999 and 2002, an additional $1 billion was allocated. From now until 2015,... $23.7 billion will be advanced to seniors, representing a solid 20% increase in the industry... .

Though current low interest rates and the 1990s real estate boom may be to blame for this rapid growth, observers believe that the RM market is about to take off due to the relentless underlying demographics of ageing. Similar projections for Europe are not readily available. However, the above actual volumes are insignificant in comparison to the potential US target Market size identified in the literature.

5. INDIAN MARKET POTENTIAL:
5.1 India-specific Characteristics of Relevance to RM :

- There are no universal social security benefits for the elderly. Formal schemes cover only about 10% of the active working population. This would significantly broaden the potential target market for RM: the 'house-rich, cash-poor'.
- A much lower proportion of urban households, and thus less room for RM.
- A much higher proportion of elders co-live with family members of subsequent generations, implying less room for RM.
- A potentially stronger bequeath motive, potentially limiting the scope for RM.
- A potential increase in the real rate of appreciation of real estate and housing prices, making RM more appealing to lenders.

- Undervaluation of real estate properties is common in order to accommodate transactions. Unaccounted money and tax evasion on property and real estate transactions
- The complexity, variety, and location-specific variations in home ownership types

a. Benami holdings/ 'Irrevocable power of attorney'
b. Leasehold/ freehold
c. Land use conversion regulations
d. Floor space regulations
e. Rent/ tenancy controls
f. Disposal of ancestral property

- There are no competitors for immediate life annuity products. This, in turn, is a result of

a. Lack of data on old age mortality rates
b. Lack of long-term treasury securities for managing interest rate risks of Annuity providers

- Because of the nascent nature of mortgage secondary markets and mortgage loan securitization in India, specific legal and taxation issues arise.

a. License/ Permission required under insurance/ banking regulation for Offering RM
b. Income tax treatment for RM lender and borrower
c. Capital gains on property
d. Reporting and provisioning by the lender as per banking/ insurance Regulation
e. Seniority of RM claims vis-à-vis other secured lenders
f. Status of RM loan in case of insolvency

References:

R. Rajagopalan (2002), Issues in Old Age social and Income Security in India, TAPMI Working Paper Series No. 2003/02, T.A. Pai Management Institute, Manipal

Huan, Clarissa and Jim Mahoney (2002) "Equity Release Mortgages", Housing Finance International, 16 (4), 29-35

Ashok Deo Burman and Samir K Barua (2003) "Home Equity Conversion: Prospects in India", Economic and Political Weekly, July 26, 3209-12

http://www.aarp.org/revmort/

Website of the American Association of Retired Persons (AARP). Provides a very detailed, downloadable "Home Made Money: A Consumer's Guide to Reverse Mortgages"

http://www.reverse.org

Website of the National Center for Home Equity Conversion, run by Ken Scholen, an advocate of Reverse Mortgage. This site provides independent information to potential consumers

http://www.reversemortgage.org

Website of the National Reverse Mortgage Lenders Association (NRMLA). Provides information of direct interest to lenders, both retail and wholesale. Gives latest information and news related to reverse mortgage industry, including profiles of a sample of borrowers, marketing aspects, detailed steps in originating loans etc.

CHAPTER VIII

Alternative Investment Funds and Real Estate Investment Funds

Ms. Dhrutvi Bhanderi; Mr. Kiran Kankotiya; Ms. Hemaxi Mistry; Mr. Deep Patel; Mr. Herin Patel

1. ALTERNATIVE INVESTMENT FUND (AIFS)

Alternative Investment Funds are a type of investment that is distinct from traditional investment instruments. It is a privately managed pooled fund. In general, institutions and HNIs invest in AIFs because large investments are required.

Alternative Investment Funds (AIFs) carry out a series of activities, beginning with the direct or indirect mobilisation of individual savings through institutions such as pension funds, insurance companies, banks, and endowments and investing them in promising enterprises, adding strategic value to portfolio companies, monitoring the investments, and exiting with the goal of realising a reasonable risk-adjusted return. AIF fund managers are fiduciaries who act in the best interests of the AIFs they manage.

This is a valuable service not only for savers and portfolio companies, but also for the Indian economy because it creates jobs, improves governance, and encourages innovation and economic growth.

Alternative Investment Funds (AIFs) include venture capital and private equity funds, which provide stable, long-term capital and typically have lives of 10 years or more. AIFs are funds with a diverse set of investment objectives and strategies. Investing in new ventures, social ventures, start-ups, growth enterprises, infrastructure, real estate, debt funds, and other investment strategies, such as angel investing through angel funds, are examples of these.

The Securities and Exchange Board of India (SEBI) regulates Alternative Investment Funds through its Alternative Investment Funds Regulations, 2012 and 2013, as well as related notifications. Reforming and aligning these and other regulations, such as those governing the tax regime, pension funds, and insurance companies, will be critical to the success of the AIF sector, paving the way for AIFs to play a much larger role in India's development, economic growth, and start-up policies.

1.1 Types of Alternative Investment Funds :

AIFS are classified into three types by the Securities and Exchange Board of India. These are their names:

1. AIFS Category 1

These funds are invested in new or growing businesses, such as start-ups, small and medium enterprises, and so on. The government encourages investment in these ventures because they benefit the economy by creating jobs and increasing output.

The following are some examples of this category:

- Infrastructure Investment Trusts
- Angel Investments
- Funds for Venture Capital
- Funds for Social Entrepreneurship

2. AIFS Category 2

This category includes funds that invest in debt and equity securities. Those funds that are not already classified as Category 1 or 3 are also included. The government makes no concessions for any investment made for Category 2 AIFS. The following are some examples of this category:

- The Fund of Funds
- Debt Funding
- Funds of Private Equity

3. AIFS Category 3

AIFs are funds that provide returns in a short period of time. To achieve their objectives, these funds employ a wide range of complex and diverse trading strategies. The government jant has made no known concessions or incentives in relation to these funds. The following are some examples of this category:

- Funds of Hedge

- Private Capital Invested in Public Equity Funds

1.2 Benefits and Drawbacks of Alternative Investment Funds

Alternative Investment Funds, like all financial instruments, have advantages and disadvantages. These are their names:

Benefits:

- Alternative investments may help to reduce the volatility that is commonly associated with traditional investments because their performance is not dependent on stock market ups and downs.
- Diversification of market strategies and investment styles is aided.
- There is a lot of room for improvement in terms of performance.

Drawbacks:

- A large investment amount is required, which small-scale investors cannot afford.
- Alternative investment funds are complex funds that require research before investing in them.

1.3 Performance of Indian AIFs industry:

As of March 31, 2022, the Indian AIF industry (alternative investment funds) had raised Rs 6.4 lakh crore in commitments, representing a 7-fold increase in the previous five years.

The minimum investment in an AIF is Rs 1 crore (Angel Funds it is Rs.25 Lakhs).

Table 1: Indian AIF Industry

Indian AIF Industry	Rs. in Crores		Growth
	31/03/17	31/03/22	
Commitments Raised	84,303.81	6,41,359.11	~ 7 times
Funds Raised	40,955.75	3,13,863.41	~ 7 times
Investments Made	35,099.15	2,84,058.64	~ 7 times
Source: www.sebi.gov.in, Monarch-Networth Research (MNCL)			

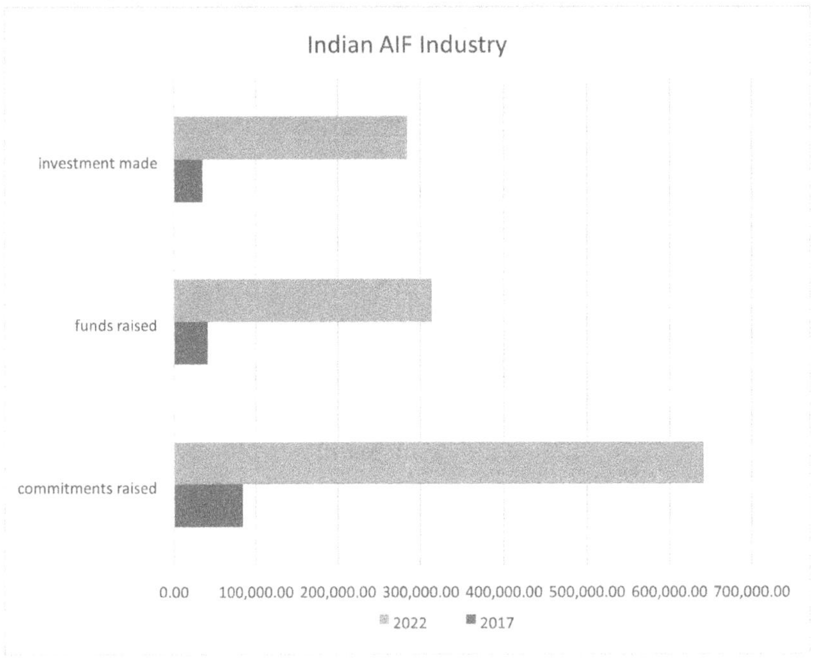

Source: Sebi.gov.in

AIF investing is rapidly expanding due to the potential for higher risk-adjusted returns via sophisticated strategies, diversification, and structural flexibility.

It is appropriate for sophisticated investors with a high risk tolerance and knowledge of asset classes.

Category – II is the biggest of all, constituting almost 80 per cent. This category comprises private equity funds, distressed funds and real estate funds.

Table 2: Composition of AIF categories

Composition of AIF categories as on 31st Mar'22	Rs. in Crores			
	Cat - I	Cat - II	Cat - III	Total
Commitments Raised	53,374.06	5,19,189.47	68,795.58	6,41,359.11
Funds Raised	29,000.10	2,23,457.30	61,406.01	3,13,863.41
Investments Made	23,798.02	1,99,451.62	60,809.00	2,84,058.64
Source: www.sebi.gov.in, Monarch-Networth Research (MNCL)				

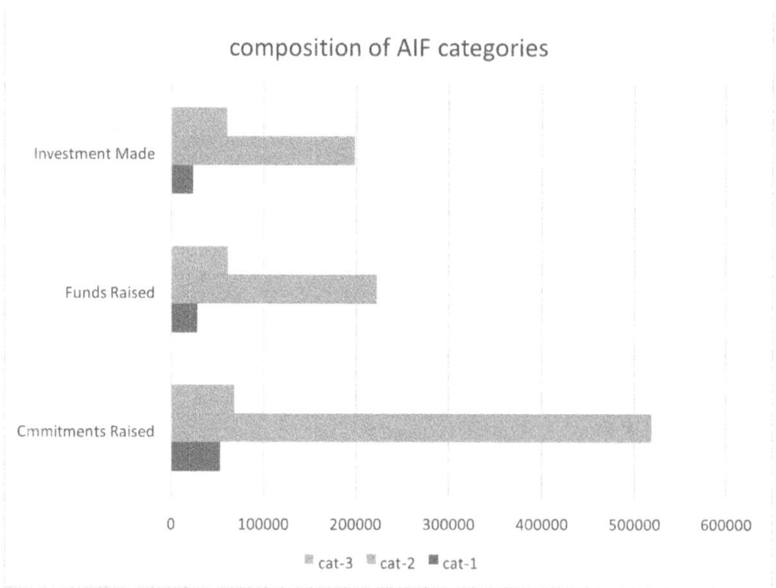

Source: Sebi.gov.in

2. REAL ESTATE INVESTMENT FUND (REIT)

A real estate investment trust (REIT) is a corporation that owns, manages, or finances income-producing real estate.

REITs, which are similar to mutual funds, pool the capital of multiple investors. Individual investors can now earn dividends from real estate investments without having to buy, manage, or finance any properties themselves.

A real estate investment trust (REIT) is a business that owns, operates, or finances rental properties.

REITs provide investors with a consistent income stream but little in the way of capital appreciation.

Most REITs are publicly traded like stocks, making them extremely liquid (unlike physical real estate investments).

REITs invest in a wide range of real estate assets, including apartment buildings, cell towers, data centres, hotels, medical facilities, offices, retail centres, and warehouses.

REITs were created in the USA by the Congress in 1960 as an amendment to the Cigar Excise Tax Extension Act. The provision allowed investors to purchase shares in commercial real estate portfolios, which were previously only available to wealthy individuals and large financial intermediaries.

Apartment complexes, data centres, healthcare facilities, hotels, infrastructure (such as fibre cables, cell towers, and energy pipelines), office buildings, retail centres, self-storage, timberland, and warehouses may be included in a REIT portfolio.

A company must follow certain provisions of the Internal Revenue Code in order to qualify as a REIT (IRC). These requirements include the long-term ownership of income-generating real estate and the distribution of income to shareholders. To qualify as a REIT, a company must meet the following requirements:

- Invest at least 75% of total assets in real estate, cash, or US Treasury bonds.
- Rents, mortgage interest on real estate, or real estate sales must account for at least 75% of gross income.
- Each year, pay a minimum of 90% of taxable income in shareholder dividends.
- Be a taxable entity such as a corporation.
- A board of directors or trustees manages the organisation.
- After its first year, it should have at least 100 shareholders.
- Have no more than five people owning more than half of the company's stock.

2.1 Types of REITs

REITs are classified into three types:

a. REITs that invest in stocks.

The vast majority of REITs are equity REITs that own and manage income-producing real estate. Rents are the primary source of revenue (not by reselling properties).

a. REITs that invest in mortgages.

Mortgage REITs lend money to property owners and operators directly through mortgages and loans or indirectly through the purchase of mortgage-backed securities. Their earnings are primarily driven by the net interest margin, which is the difference between the interest they earn on mortgage loans and the cost of funding these loans. Because of this model, they are potentially sensitive to interest rate increases.

c. REITs that are hybrids.

These REITs employ both equity and mortgage REIT investment strategies.

Table 3: REIT Types Comparison

Type of REIT	Holdings
Equity	Owns and operates income-producing real estate
Mortgage	Holds mortgages on real property
Hybrid	Owns properties and holds mortgages

REITs are further classified according to how their shares are purchased and held:

- REITs that are publicly traded.

Shares of publicly traded REITs are traded the stock exchange, where individual investors can buy and sell them. They are governed by the Securities and Exchange Board of India.

- Non-traded public REITs.

Although these REITs are registered with the SEBI, they do not trade on national securities exchanges. As a result, they are less liquid than publicly traded real estate investment trusts. Nonetheless, they are more stable because they are not affected by market fluctuations.

- REITs that are privately held.

These REITs are not SEC-registered and do not trade on national securities exchanges.

Private REITs are generally only available to institutional investors.

2.2 Advantages and Disadvantages of REITs:

Advantages:

- Liquidity
- Diversification
- Transparency
- Stable cash flow through dividends
- Attractive risk-adjusted returns

Disadvantages:

- Low growth
- Dividends are taxed as regular income
- Subject to market risk
- Potential for high management and transaction fees

Chart 1: Performance of the Indian REITs Industry

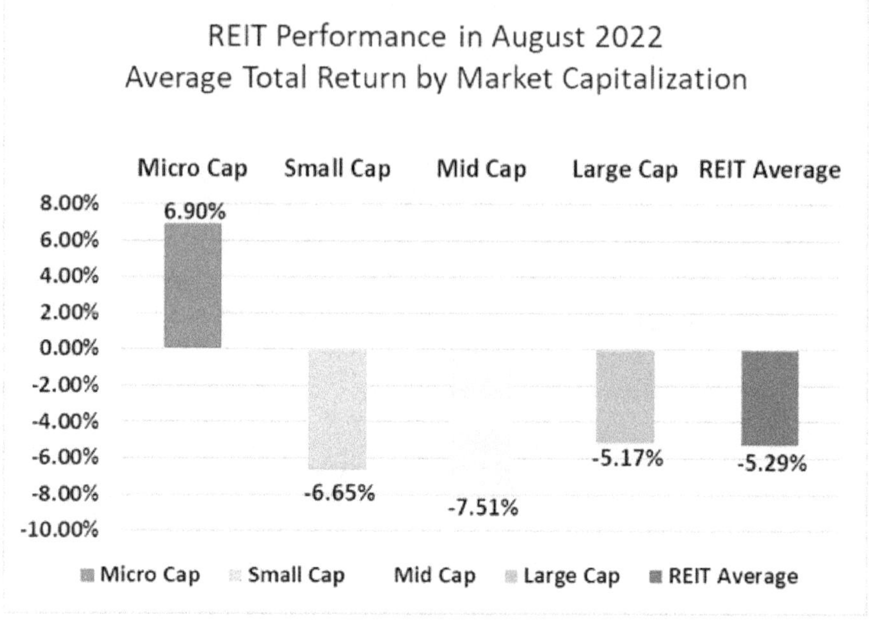

Source: https://seekingalpha.com/article/4554229-state-of-reits-november-2022-edition

Summary

- The REIT sector has experienced losses in six of the first eight months of 2022, including a -5.29 percent total return in August.
- In August, micro cap REITs (+6.9 percent) outperformed large caps (-5.17 percent), small caps (-6.65 percent), and mid caps (-7.51 percent).
- In August, only 15.06 percent of REIT securities had a positive total return.
- Shopping Center (+3.21%) and Self-Storage (+0.78%) REITs remained profitable and led all property types in August. Office (-12.33%) and Diversified (-9.24%) REITs underperformed.
- During August, the average REIT NAV discount increased from -15.24 percent to -20.28 percent.
- The median NAV discount increased as well, from -12.67 percent to -20.04 percent.

Table 4: REIT Performance

REIT Performance August 2022		
Property Type	Average Return	Number of REITs
Office	-12.33%	21
Diversified	-9.24%	16
Land	-8.72%	3
Malls	-8.62%	4
Manufactured Housing	-8.46%	3
Multifamily	-6.69%	14
Single Family Housing	-6.32%	2
Triple Net	-6.27%	18
Timber	-5.61%	4
Advertising	-5.61%	2
Industrial	-5.45%	12
Casino	-5.33%	2
Health Care	-4.87%	16
Hotel	-3.31%	16
Data Center	-1.45%	3
Infrastructure	-0.61%	6
Self-Storage	0.78%	6
Shopping Center	3.21%	20
REIT Average	-5.29%	168

Source: Seekingalpha.com

References:

economictimes. (2022, June 29). Retrieved November 8, 2022, from economictimes.indiatimes.com: https://economictimes.indiatimes.com/markets/stocks/news

Grow. (2022, march 29). Retrieved november 04, 2022, from grow.com: https://groww.in/blog/all-about-alternate-investment-funds-aifs

investopedia. (2022, april 4). Retrieved november 6, 2022, from www.investopedia.com: https://www.investopedia.com/terms/r/reit.asp

seekingalpha. (2022, september 20). Retrieved november 8, 2022, from seekingalpha.com: https://seekingalpha.com/article/4542048-the-state-of-reits-september-2022-edition

CHAPTER IX

Impact of GST on Small and Medium Enterprises (SMEs) in India

Ms. Shrusti Patel; Ms. Suman Rakholiya; Ms. Shobha Srivastava; Ms. Aishwarya Sonawane; Ms. Priya Yadav; Mr. Shubham Yadav

1. INTRODUCTION

Small and medium enterprises have been considered as the primary growth drive of the Indian economy for decades. It is further evident from the fact that today we have around 3 million small and medium enterprises in Indian contributing almost 50% of the industrial output and 42% of Indian total export. For a developing country like Indian and it is demographic diversity, small and medium enterprises have emerged as the leading employment generating sector and has provided balanced development across sector. Under the GST bill, no entry tax will be charged for goods manufactured or sold in any part of India. They have also positive or negative impact on GST on small and medium enterprises. GST will reduce the logistic cost of the company production non bulk goods by 20%.

1.1 Overview of GST:-

- Implement on 1ˢᵗ July 2017
- Unified indirect taxation system replaced by many IT
- One country, one market, one tax
- Tax rate- 0%, 5%, 12%, 18%, 28%
- Reduce the complication of taxes and improve the system of indirect taxes
- Upgrade their record keeping system
- Regulate unorganized sector

2. CONCEPTUAL FRAMEWORK

2.1 What is the Goods and Services Tax?

The goods and services tax is a value-added tax levied on most goods and services sold for domestic consumption. The GST is paid by consumers, but it is remitted to the government by the businesses selling the goods and services.

The goods and services tax is an indirect federal sales tax that is applied to the cost of certain goods and services. The business adds the GST to the price of the product, and a customer who buys the product pays the sales price inclusive of the GST. The GST portion is collected by the business or seller and forwarded to the government. It is also referred to as Value-Added Tax in some countries.

2.2 Types of goods and services tax:-

Integrated Goods and Services Tax or IGST

The Integrated Goods and Services Tax or IGST is a tax under the GST regime that is applied on the interstate (between 2 states) supply of goods and/or services as well as on imports and exports.

The IGST is governed by the IGST Act. Under IGST, the body responsible for collecting the taxes is the Central Government. After the collection of taxes, it is further divided among the respective states by the Central Government.

For instance, if a trader from West Bengal has sold goods to a customer in Karnataka worth Rs.5,000, then IGST will be applicable as the transaction is an interstate transaction. If the rate of GST charged on the goods is 18%, the trader will charge Rs.5,900 for the goods. The IGST collected is Rs.900, which will be going to the Central Government.

State Goods and Services Tax or SGST

The State Goods and Services Tax or SGST is a tax under the GST regime that is applicable on intrastate (within the same state) transactions. In the case of an intrastate supply of goods and/or services, both State GST and Central GST are levied.

However, the State GST or SGST is levied by the state on the goods and/or services that are purchased or sold within the state. It is governed by the SGST Act. The revenue earned through SGST is solely claimed by the respective state government.

For instance, if a trader from West Bengal has sold goods to a customer in West Bengal worth Rs.5,000, then the GST applicable on the transaction will be partly CGST and partly SGST. If the rate of GST charged is 18%, it will be divided equally in the form of 9% CGST and 9% SGST. The total amount to be charged by the trader, in this case, will be Rs.5,900. Out of the revenue earned from GST under the head of SGST, i.e. Rs.450, will go to the West Bengal state government in the form of SGST.

Central Goods and Services Tax or CGST

Just like State GST, the Central Goods and Services Tax of CGST is a tax under the GST regime that is applicable on intrastate (within the same state) transactions. The CGST is governed by the CGST Act. The revenue earned from CGST is collected by the Central Government.

As mentioned in the above instance, if a trader from West Bengal has sold goods to a customer in West Bengal worth Rs.5,000, then the GST applicable on the transaction will be partly CGST and partly SGST. If the rate of GST charged is 18%, it will be divided equally in the form of 9% CGST and 9% SGST. The total amount to be charged by the trader, in this case, will be Rs.5,900. Out of the revenue earned from GST under the head of CGST, i.e. Rs.450, will go to the Central Government in the form of CGST

2.3 Small and Medium size Enterprises:

Small and mid-size enterprises (SMEs) are businesses that maintain assets, revenue or a number of employees below a certain threshold.

In the case of small enterprises:

The manufacturing sector's investment in plant & machinery should be more than 25 lakh rupees and less than 5 crore rupees.

The service sector's investment in the equipment should be more than 10 lakh rupees and less than 2 crore rupees.

In the case of medium enterprises:

The manufacturing sector's investment in plant & machinery should be more than 5 crore rupees and less than 10 crore rupees.

The service sector's investment in the equipment should be more than 2 crore rupees and less than 5 crore rupees.

2.4 The importance of SMEs

Utilization of Local Resources

Opening up of small and medium-sized businesses in rural areas or small towns helps in better utilization of resources in that particular area. If a town is rich in iron ore mines, then factories will open up for the effective utilization of that resource.

Employment Generation

SMEs are the best solution to unemployment in any country. It provides job opportunities for local people. Especially, in developing countries like India, where unemployment has been a major problem, these businesses provide relief.

Opportunities to New Entrepreneurs

The major role of SMEs in any country is to cultivate new entrepreneurs. Since small businesses are easier to set up and require less capital, it creates a perfect option for young entrepreneurs to test their skills and grow.

Development of Local Areas

The development of an area largely depends upon the number of businesses it has. Setting up small businesses helps in providing employment to the local population and removing regional imbalances.

Improvement Of The Quality of Life

SMEs help the locals by providing them jobs. This increases the per capita income of the household which improves their quality of life (*Goods and Services Tax (GST): Definition, Types, and How It's Calculated*, n.d.).

3. POSITIVE IMPACTS OF GST ON SMES

3.1 Launching a new business becomes easier

Under the previous tax regime, if your business had operations across multiple states, you would need to register for VAT with each state's sales tax department in order to carry out business activities there. The fact that every state had different tax rules complicated the entire process, and business owners had to pay multiple procedural fees for VAT registration. Under GST, the registration is centralized and the rules are uniform for all the states across the country. All you have to do is complete and submit an online form to obtain a GSTIN (GST Identification Number). Launching a new business, and subsequently expanding it, will be comparatively easier under the GST regime.

3.2 The entire process of taxation becomes simpler

The prime reason GST is implemented is to remove cascading taxation. It reduces the complications caused by the overlap between Central taxes (Excise duty, customs duty, service tax, etc.) and State taxes (VAT, purchase tax, luxury tax, etc.), because it levies a uniform tax on goods and services all over India. The taxes on goods and services levied under VAT, purchase tax, and luxury tax will now be merged into one single tax with one common return. If you've spent a large portion of your time on managing multiple taxes, you can relax under the new regime because filing and paying taxes is easier with the GSTN portal.

3.3 The distinction between goods and services will be eliminated

Previously, businesses providing both goods and services had to calculate the VAT and service taxes individually. GST eases the process by removing the distinction between goods and services; tax will be calculated for the final total, not individual products or services. This will help SMEs take advantage of the tax incentives for payment on the procurement of input goods and services (like import, interstate and local purchases, and telephone services).

3.4 Increased threshold limits for new businesses

Under the current regime, businesses with a moderate annual turnover (Rs.5 lakh in some states and Rs.10 lakh in other states) are supposed to register and make payments for VAT. Under GST, this burden is eliminated for many businesses, since a business does not have to register or pay if its annual turnover is less than Rs.20 lakh (Rs.10 lakh in North Eastern states). Also, under the composition scheme, businesses with turnover between Rs.20-Rs.50 lakh will pay GST at a lower rate. This should have a positive effect on startups and other small businesses by relieving them from tax burdens.

(*Impact of GST on Small and Medium Enterprises (SMEs) | Zoho*, n.d.)

4. NEGATIVE IMPACTS OF GST ON SMES

4.1 Multiple registrations for Pan-India businesses

Under the new regime, a business will have to register online for GST in every state involved in its sales process. If your business delivers goods across 5 states, then you'll have to register for GST in those 5 states to carry out your business activities. Since the entire registration process takes place online, small business owners who are not used to working online might not find the transition easy.

4.2 Returns must be filed on a monthly basis

Under GST, there will be around 36 returns in a fiscal year. GST returns will also require you to close your books on a monthly basis, which, will take a lot of time. Also, until you've filed the relevant returns, you cannot claim refunds and your customers cannot claim tax credit for the goods they bought from you. Should you miss a single return, you'll be penalized Rs.100/- a day and your compliance rating on the GSTN portal will be reduced.

4.3 Registration will be mandatory for e-commerce suppliers and operators

Businesses carrying out activities related to e-commerce should register under GST irrespective of their annual turnover rate. Unlike other types of businesses, e-commerce firms will not be eligible for threshold exemptions or for the Composition Scheme (which allows firms to file their tax returns on a quarterly basis instead of 3 times a year and pay taxes at a much lower rate).

Also, e-commerce firms should register for GST in every single state where they supply goods (*Impact of GST on Small and Medium Enterprises*

(SMEs) | Zoho, n.d.).

5.IMMEDIATE GST EFFECT ON ECONOMY:

5.1 Simplified Tax Structure

The country's tax structure has been streamlined due to GST. Since GST is a single tax, calculating taxes at various supply chain points has become more straightforward. Therefore, GST impact on India can be considered positive. Customers and manufacturers can both see how much tax they'll be charged and how it'll be calculated this way. It is also possible to avoid the difficulties of dealing with tax officers and authorities.

5.2 Support for SMEs

Small and medium-sized businesses can now register under the GST Composition Scheme. They pay taxes based on their annual revenue under this arrangement. As a result, firms with annual revenue of Rs. 1.5 crores are only needed to pay 1% GST. Other businesses with a turnover of Rs. 50 lakh are also required to pay GST at a rate of 6%.

5.3 Additional funding for production

The reduction in the overall taxable amount is another effect of GST on Indian economy. This money saved may be re-invested in the manufacturing process to boost output.

5.4 Elimination of cascading effect of taxes

The state and central governments' taxes have been combined under GST. This has eliminated the tax cascade effect, lowering the burden on both the buyer and the seller. So, even though it appears like you are paying a large amount of tax, you are paying fewer hidden taxes.

5.5 Improved operations across India

Tax barriers such as toll plazas and checkpoints can now be avoided. Previously, this caused issues, such as harm to unpreserved items during transportation. As a result, producers had to maintain buffer stock on hand to compensate for the losses. Their profit was limited by the overhead expenditures of storage and warehousing. These issues have been mitigated by a unified taxing system catering to the positive impact of GST. They may now readily move their wares throughout India. As a result, their operations across India have improved.

5.6 Increasing output

The overall tax component is about 30% of the product cost, according to the Indian retail industry. Taxes have decreased due to GST effects in India. As a result, the final customer pays lower taxes. The reduction in tax burden has boosted retail and other businesses' output and growth.

5.7 Increase in exports

The customs charge on products exported has been decreased. The GST impact in India has resulted in the reduction of the cost of production in local markets. All of these reasons have boosted the country's export rate. When it comes to developing their companies worldwide, firms have grown more competitive.

The introduction of GST has aided in the consolidation of state and federal taxes. The cascading effect of numerous taxes has been reduced as a result of this. As a result, the tax burden on businesses and consumers has decreased. Also, the number of taxpayers has grown, resulting in a considerable increase in tax income. The whole tax system is now simpler to administer. Furthermore, small and medium-sized firms can expand their operations. It is believed that the positive impact of GST would assist more Indian businesses in entering overseas markets.

5.8 What is the effect of GST on consumer?

- Consumers will now have to pay higher taxes on products and services they purchase, based on the short-term effects.

- The bulk of necessary consumables will be taxed at the same rate or a higher rate. The benefits or positive impact of GST on the average person are numerous.
- Small-scale businesses must also pay the expense of compliance, which may result in higher costs for their goods, impacting consumers.
- GST effects in India have several long-term advantages. With the reduction in due taxes for consumer goods makers such as Fast-moving consumer goods or FMCG, the automobile industry will be forced to lower the pricing of its products. The clients will be able to pay less when attempting to obtain these services due to this.
- A reduction in pricing will instantly increase demand, accelerating the production cycle and increasing profitability. Both the buyer and the seller will eventually save money, and the economy will benefit as well.
- A jump in output will also create the path for growth, which will result in more jobs and more revenue catering to the GST impacts. This not only expands opportunities for the average person but also helps the economy.
- The introduction of GST necessitates the creation of an invoice for the purchase of any goods or services.
- The possibility of black money and corruption will be reduced with a good billing system. For an average person in India, these have been troublesome elements (*Effect of GST on the Indian Economy*, n.d.).

5.9 BENEFITS OF GST IMPLEMENTATION

Key benefits of the GST announcement are detailed below:

1. The GST system will create a common national market that boosts foreign investment.
2. The cascading effect of taxation will be mitigated.
3. There will be uniformity in laws, rates of tax, and procedures across states.
4. The GST regime is expected to boost manufacturing activities and exports. This would, in turn, generate more employment and lead to the growth of the economy.
5. Indian products would be more competitive in the international markets.

6. The GST system is likely to improve the overall investment climate in India.

7. Uniformity in the rates of SGST and IGST will reduce tax evasion to a large extent.

8. The average sales burden experienced by companies is expected to come down, thereby increasing consumption and boosting subsequent production of goods.

9. GST is a simpler system of taxation with smaller number of exemptions.

10. There are automated and simplified methods for processes such as registration, refunds, returns of GST, tax payments, etc.

11. All interactions will be handled by the common GSTN website.

12. The input tax credit process will be more accurate and transparent, as electronic matching will be performed.

13. The final price of most goods will be lower when taxation is at the New GST rates. There will also be a seamless input tax credit flow between the manufacturer, retailer, and supplier of service.

14. A huge segment of small-scale retailers may be either exempt from tax or may benefit from low tax rates based on the compounding scheme. Consumers will further benefit if purchases are made from these small retailers (*History of GST in India - Benefits of GST Implementation*, n.d.).

6. LATEST GROWTH AND DEVELOPMENT

6.1 GST: A perfect tool for SME growth:

The Government of India commemorated July 1, 2018 — the first anniversary of the Goods and Services Tax — as GST Day. During the past year, the government earned an estimated Rs 7.41 lakh crore from the new indirect tax and it is confident that collections will exceed Rs 13 lakh crore in the current financial year. I will be bold enough to say that we are well on course to reach that number.

Looking back, the implementation of the 'one nation-one tax' regime was not easy for the micro, small and medium enterprises (MSME) sector, which faced problems with cash flows and GST compliance. The bumpy ride is now behind us and I am equally confident that the 48 lakh MSMEs registered with the Udyog Aadhaar Memorandum (UAM) Portal as of July 2018 — thanks mainly to the 'Make in India' initiative — will significantly increase their share of GST in FY19.

On the positive side, the replacement of as many as 17 levies and numerous cesses with a single tax has made tax filing simpler and systematic, and also streamlined processes. This has enabled MSMEs to channelise manpower and other resources towards business growth and development.

Apart from the above, GST has had a major impact on old-school accounting methods that were prone to errors. The new tax has forced enterprises to adopt digital technology and improve business efficiency. This is benefiting companies as well as their suppliers, vendors and customers.

With an increased transparency in accounting procedures we have witnessed a surge in financial participation from established institutions. Today, there is far more flexibility in business cycles with a lowered cost of borrowing options for MSME's.

Besides, March is a low activity month for MSMEs which channelise most of their efforts towards tallying books of accounts and filing taxes. With GST, however, enterprises have to check their books regularly. What this means is that MSMEs can identify defaulters, ensure faster payments and streamline their ledgers.

Another benefit of GST is that MSMEs can go beyond their geographical state and expand their business anywhere in the country. Enterprises no longer have to worry about dealing with complex taxes applicable in different states. In that sense, GST is creating new business and employment opportunities.

GST will usher in an era of growth in the MSME sector and transform the way enterprises operate and do business. In the long run, this will have a positive impact on the economy (*Gst: GST: A Perfect Tool for SME Growth - The Economic Times*, n.d.).

References:

Effect of GST on the Indian Economy. (n.d.). Retrieved November 21, 2022, from https://khatabook.com/blog/impact-of-gst-on-the-indian-economy/

Goods and Services Tax (GST): Definition, Types, and How It's Calculated. (n.d.). Retrieved November 21, 2022, from https://www.investopedia.com/terms/g/gst.asp

Gst: GST: A perfect tool for SME growth—The Economic Times. (n.d.). Retrieved November 21, 2022, from https://m.economictimes.com/small-biz/sme-sector/gst-a-perfect-tool-for-sme-growth/amp_articleshow/68125258.cms

History of GST in India—Benefits of GST Implementation. (n.d.). Retrieved November 21, 2022, from https://www.bankbazaar.com/tax/history-of-gst.html

Impact of GST on Small and Medium Enterprises (SMEs) | Zoho. (n.d.). Retrieved November 21, 2022, from https://www.zoho.com/books/gst-articles/impact-of-gst-on-smes.html

CHAPTER X

Microfinance in India: Issues, Challenge and Success Factors

Ms. Ayushi Randeri; Ms. Krisha Shah; Ms. Mitali Shiroya; Ms. Vrutti Sonani;
Mr. Pranay Valand; Ms. Anjali Thatipamula

1. INTRODUCTION

Microfinance is defined as any activity that involves the provision of financial services such as credit, savings, and insurance to low-income individuals who fall just above the nationally-defined poverty line, and to poor individuals who fall below that line, with the intention of creating social value. The creation of social value encompasses the alleviation of poverty and the broader impact of improving livelihood opportunities through the provision of capital for micro enterprise, insurance, and savings for risk management and consumption smoothing. Microfinance is provided in India by a wide range of actors using a variety of delivery methods. Since the establishment of the Grameen Bank in Bangladesh, various actors have endeavoured to provide the poor with innovative access to financial services. Governments have piloted national programmes, non-governmental organisations (NGOs) have raised donor funds for on-lending, and some banks have partnered with public organisations or made small inroads in providing these services themselves. This has led to a rather broad definition of microfinance as any activity that provides financial services to poor and low-income individuals. Microfinance encompasses a variety of activities, such as group lending, the provision of savings and insurance, capacity building, and agriculture business development services. Regardless of the type of activity, the overarching objective shared by all microfinance providers is the creation of social value.

1. MICROFINANCE DEFINITION

According to the International Labor Organization (ILO), microfinance is an economic development strategy involving the provision of financial services to low-income clients through institutions.

The National Microfinance Taskforce of India (1999) defines microfinance as "provision of savings, credit, and other financial services and products of very small amounts to the poor in rural and semi-urban areas in order to increase their income levels and improve their living standards."

3. EVOLUTION OF MICROFINANCE

- Nobel Prize winner Muhammad Yunus (2006) introduced the concept of microfinance to Bangladesh in the form of the Grameen Bank.

- Microfinance in India evolved with the founding of SIDBI. In 1992, NABARD introduced the concept of microfinance and established a link between Self-Help Groups (DHGs), Non-Governmental Organizations (NGOs), and Banks.

- NABARD launched the Micro-Enterprise Development Programme (MEDP) for skill development in 2006.

4. FEATURES OF MICROFINANCE

- The borrowers are low-income groups.
- The loans are for small amounts.
- The loans are without collaterals.
- The loans are generally taken for income-generating activities, although loans are also provided for consumption, housing and other purposes.
- The tenure of the loans is short.
- The frequency of repayment is greater than for traditional commercial loans.

5. NEED FOR MICROFINANCE

- As a result of the substantial costs associated with managing borrower accounts, banks have been hesitant to provide microfinancing to poor individuals with little or no cash income.
- The poor have no or very few assets to offer as collateral security for bank loans. Therefore, banks fear having limited recourse against

delinquent borrowers.

- Before providing microcredit to the majority of the poor, banks require proper proof of identity and address, as the majority of the poor do not have bank accounts.
- Lack of knowledge, initiative, and collateral assets are obstacles to obtaining credit from banks. People require microfinance to conduct their economic endeavours in a commercial manner.
- Microfinance is necessary for economic growth and national transformation. Microfinance is required to eradicate poverty and accelerate national development.
- Microfinance is required to meet the people's life cycle, emergency, and investment needs.
- Microfinance is necessary for women's economic and social empowerment through development.

6. TYPES OF MICROFINANCE COMPANIES OPERATING IN INDIA

- Joint Liability Group (JLG)
- Self Help Group (SHG)
- The Grameen Bank Model
- Rural Co-operatives

7. CHALLENGES FOR MFI IN INDIA

- Financial illiteracy
- Lack of information
- Inability to generate funds
- Weak governance
- High Interest Rate
- Regional Imbalances
- Low Outreach
- Client Retention and Debt Management

8. REGULATORY FRAMEWORK FOR MFIS

- The regulatory framework of a country can have a significant impact on microfinance's viability. The forms of legal organisation, exemptions, registration requirements, interest rate caps, capitalization, etc. available to an institution are all determined by the legal framework.

- Regulations of microfinance refer to the body of laws that govern microfinance. Compliance with these regulations is currently being enforced by supervision. Deposit-taking financial service providers require prudential oversight. Regulation contributes to long-term sustainability, even if MFIs are initially safe under it.

9. AIM OF SUPPORTIVE REGULATORY FRAMEWORK

- To provide services on a sustainable basis in accordance with uniform, shared performance criteria.
- To encourage the regulatory authority to develop prudential regulations and staffing levels that are tailored to the operational and risk profile of the institution.

9.1 Regulatory bodies for MFI in India

- Microfinance Institutions Network (MFIN)
- Reserve Bank of India.

9.2 About MFIN

- Microfinance Institutions Network (MFIN) is a network of microfinance institutions in Asia. Its member organisations are the nation's leading microfinance institutions.
- MFIN's primary goal is to promote the robust growth of the microfinance industry by promoting Responsible Lending, Client Protection, Good Governance, and a Supportive Regulatory Environment.
- Through microfinance, MFIN collaborates closely with regulators and other key stakeholders and actively participates in the larger dialogue on financial inclusion.
- RBI regulates MFIs and MFINs are represented by the primary representative body, MFIN.

9.3 RBI regulations for MFI

MFIs are required to have at least 85 percent of their net assets in qualifying assets that meet the following criteria:

- Minimum Net Owned Fund (NOF) of Rs. 5 crore (North-East Region, Rs.2 Cr.)
- 85 percent of MFI's total assets are comprised of qualifying assets. A qualifying asset is a loan that meets the following requirements:
- The loan is extended to borrowers whose annual household income in rural areas does not exceed Rs 100,000, and in non-rural areas, Rs 160,000.
- The loan cannot exceed Rs. 60,000 in the initial cycle and Rs. 100,000 in subsequent cycles.
- The borrower's total debt does not exceed Rs.100,000.
- Education and medical expenses are not included when calculating total debt. When the loan amount exceeds Rs.15,000, the minimum loan term is 24 months, and the borrower may prepay without penalty.
- To extend loans without collateral. At least fifty percent of MFIs' total loans should be for income generation, allowing the remaining fifty percent to be used for other purposes such as housing repairs, education, and other emergencies.
- The borrower has the option of repaying the loan in weekly, biweekly, or monthly instalments.
- Within the prescribed cap limits, the average interest rate on loans during a fiscal year cannot exceed the average borrowing cost during that fiscal year plus the margin.
- The interest rate on individual loans may exceed 26%; however, the difference between the minimum and maximum interest rate on individual loans cannot exceed 4%.
- The pricing of loans must include only three components: a) processing fees not to exceed one percent of the gross loan amount, b) the interest rate, and c) the insurance premium.

There shouldn't be any late payment penalties. No security deposit or margin is required. Capital requirement (CRAR): 15% of its risk-weighted total assets.

10. ADVANTAGES OF MICROFINANCE

1. **It enables individuals to provide for their families more effectively.**

Microfinance contributes to a greater degree of resilience in the developing world. Even when families are able to work their way out of poverty, it typically takes only one negative event to send them back into poverty. Frequently, a problem with health care causes a return to poverty. By allowing entrepreneurs to become more resilient through their own efforts in their own business, they are given the opportunity to endure economic hardship.

The majority of households that take advantage of microfinance opportunities in developing nations are classified as living in "extreme poverty." This is defined as surviving on $1.25 or less per day, although some definitions extend this to $2 or more per day. Approximately 80 percent of that amount is allocated to the acquisition or production of food resources.

By providing microfinance products that can be repaid with the remaining 20 percent, more households have the opportunity to increase their current income-generating potential.

2. **It gives individuals access to credit.**

Muhammad Yunus, who is commonly regarded as the modern father of microfinance, once gave $27 from his own pocket to bamboo chair-making women because he observed how the cycle of debt affected their work. Due to the inherent risks, the majority of banks will not extend loans to borrowers without credit or collateral, yet those in poverty lack credit and collateral.

3. **By providing people with access to small amounts of credit through microfinance, poverty can be eradicated rapidly.**

Yunus has always held that access to credit is a basic human right. There may be some financial institutions that disagree with his evaluation. Yet, without credit, it can be difficult, if not impossible, for a poor person to pursue an idea that could one day yield a substantial profit. Microfinance enables this endeavour.

4. **It assists those who are frequently neglected by society.**

In many developing nations, women are typically the primary recipients of microloans. Up to ninety-five percent of microfinance institutions' loan products are extended to women. Those with disabilities, the unemployed, and even those who beg for their basic needs are recipients of microfinance products that empower them to take charge of their lives.

Even in the developed world, women occupy key positions in business leadership. Catalyst reports that companies with female board directors can achieve up to 66 percent higher returns on invested capital and 42 percent higher sales returns than those with only male board members.

Additionally, women develop others more frequently in entrepreneurial roles. This can be achieved through coaching, feedback, or investments. Even in developed nations, women helping women is an economic force that cannot be stopped by poverty.

5. **It provides a better overall rate of loan repayment than conventional banking products.**

When individuals are empowered, they are more likely to avoid loan default. Women are statistically more likely to repay a loan than men, which is yet another reason why microfinance institutions target women. In addition, for many individuals who receive a microloan, it is their only real opportunity to escape poverty, so they don't mess things up.

Zenger Folkman published a gender-specific survey regarding ratings of high integrity and honesty in leadership positions. The mean percentile of women exhibiting these characteristics was 55%, while for men it was only 48%. The bottom line in business is that integrity matters. Microfinance institutions have acknowledged this and reached out to women as a result.

As a result of this strategy, many developing nations are reevaluating the role women should play in society. Instead of treating women as second-class citizens or with the "barefoot in the kitchen and pregnant" mentality that was prevalent in the past, the success of women in bringing their households out of poverty is proof that not only do women have the initiative to get things done, but they also produce consistent results.

Due to these factors, microfinance institutions experience overall repayment rates of greater than 98 percent, despite the fact that several accounts may be delinquent at any given time.

6. **It gives families the opportunity to provide their children with an education.**

Children living in poverty are more likely to have missed school days or to be unenrolled. This is because the majority of poor families are employed in the agricultural sector. Families require their children to be employed and productive in order to meet their financial needs. Receiving microfinancing products reduces the risk of insufficient funding, thereby increasing the likelihood that children will remain in school.

This is particularly crucial for families with girls. When girls receive only eight years of formal education, they are four times less likely to marry before the age of twenty. They are less likely to become pregnant as adolescents. In turn, this increases the likelihood that girls will complete their education, obtain a well-paying job, or pursue further education.

7. **It creates opportunities for future investments.**

The issue with poverty is that it is a self-perpetuating cycle. When there is not enough money, there is not enough food. When there is an absence of clean water, living conditions are unsanitary. When individuals are malnourished, they are less likely to work. A lack of sanitation increases the likelihood of illness, resulting in lost work days.

This is altered by microfinance, which makes more money available. When basic needs are met, families can invest in better wells, sanitation, and health care, as well as afford the time it may take to receive it.

As these fundamental needs are satisfied, there are fewer disruptions to the routine. People can be more efficient. Children can attend school more regularly. Better healthcare is available. This reduces the average family size because there are more survival guarantees in place.

When this occurs, there will be a greater likelihood of future investments because there will be greater confidence in the ability to meet basic needs.

8. **This method is sustainable.**

What is the risk associated with a $100 loan? Some investors might pay that much for a decent meal. Yet $100 could be sufficient for an entrepreneur in a developing nation to escape poverty. This modest amount of working capital is sufficient because it is essentially negligible.

In the event of a default, the interest and high repayment rates of other microloans will compensate. Then, repayments are re-invested back into the community so that the benefits of microfinance can continue to grow. Each repayment becomes the basis for a potential future loan.

This is the reason why numerous microfinance products have relatively high interest rates. Some institutions may charge the equivalent of a 20% APR, whereas others charge interest rates that exceed 800%. Although interest rates are high, recipients are invested in the success of these products because virtually all institutions reinvest repayments into new loans aimed at the most vulnerable households in developing countries.

9. It can create legitimate jobs.

Additionally, microfinance enables entrepreneurs in developing nations to generate new employment opportunities. When more people are able to work and earn a living, the local economy as a whole benefits because more money is available to flow through local businesses and services.

Microfinance's contribution to job creation is not restricted to the entrepreneurial level. Over 21,000 people are employed by Grameen Bank in Bangladesh, and their primary financial products are related to microfinance. This industry creates tens of thousands of jobs whose sole purpose is to help people escape poverty.

10. It encourages individuals to save.

Microloans are an integral part of microfinance, but so are savings accounts. When a person's basic needs are met, their natural inclination is to save the remainder of their earnings for a future emergency. This creates the possibility for more investments and, ultimately, an increase in income for those in the developing world.

When products are extended, microfinance institutions have witnessed an extraordinary number of savings. Bank Rakyat Indonesia's Unit Desai has 28 million savers but only 3 million microloan borrowers.

Saving is not always observed, especially among borrowers, but it is part of the microfinance process. Small loans make modest financial improvements for low-income households. In reality, the difference between earning $1.90 and $2.30 per day is negligible, but by definition, this amount lifts a person out of extreme poverty.

Instead of large improvements, microfinance enables small ones. When enough of these improvements are made, this industry will provide a secure place for people to store their money.

11. It alleviates stress.

There is a valid argument that some microloans are used to cover personal expenses rather than business needs. Some individuals use these loans to pay their bills or to purchase food. It's a fact. However, without this product, it would be impossible to pay bills or purchase food. Therefore, even if it is not always used for business, it still serves a purpose by reducing stress.

When it comes to poverty, stress cannot be underestimated. Even in developing nations, the tribulations of poverty can be overwhelming. It motivates individuals to seek out unhealthy coping mechanisms. In some cases, it may even lead to the dissolution of families.

Sometimes childbirth is a coping mechanism for poverty because an additional pair of hands represents an additional opportunity for income. By reducing these stress indicators, households can concentrate on the task at hand to provide for themselves, despite the fact that their net income levels may not increase in the near future.

12. It allows individuals to feel as though they have value.

It is impossible to ignore the sensation of receiving a credit product for the first time. It is a feeling of accomplishment. That you are a credible individual because you have been granted credit. This sentiment is universal, even in the developed world. When a person feels that they matter, they undergo fundamental transformation. Instead of focusing on how to merely survive, they should seek ways to thrive.

This brings up the strain that poverty places on individuals. When people are approved for a microloan for the first time, they frequently have the same reaction as Steve Martin in The Jerk when he discovered his name in the phone book.

Consequently, Yunus considers credit to be a fundamental right. Without credit, survival is frequently the best-case scenario. There is hope that anything is possible with credit.

13. **It offers substantial economic benefits even if income levels remain unchanged.**

The benefits of participating in a microfinance programme include improved nutrition, increased consumption, and consumption smoothing. There is also an effect that cannot be quantified when women are granted the authority to do something in their society that they would not normally be permitted to do. As expenditures occur, these benefits extend to those who may not be participating in the programme, thereby benefiting the entire community.

The most significant shortcoming of microfinance is that the effects of increasing income levels for the poor are frequently dubious. Although microfinance products increase the likelihood of income accumulation and savings, they also increase the likelihood of incurring additional debt, which could potentially perpetuate cycles of poverty indefinitely.

Although some may view consumption negatively, those who have gone without for so long will view increased consumption as an indication that conditions are improving. Consumption smoothing enables an entire community to realise microfinance's potential benefits.

11. DISADVANTAGES MICROFINANCE

1. Harsh repayment criteria

In the absence of legitimate working protocols and compliances, Microfinance Companies may adopt a harsh repayment strategy that no one would choose during a financial crisis. Microfinance institutions are not an exception to the rule that easy credit comes with strict terms. Since these businesses operate under stringent regulations, they may engage in unethical customer repayment manipulation.

2. Small Loan amount

In contrast to conventional financial institutions, Microfinance Companies offer smaller loan amounts. Since these banks do not require collateral against the credit, it is practically impossible for them to issue a large loan.

3. *High-interest rate*

Another issue with Microfinance Companies was their inability to provide low-interest loans. This is because they do not follow the footprint of conventional banks, where the accumulation of funds is simple. In addition, they must borrow money from these banks in order to execute properly and allocate a portion of it for risk management. Consequently, their operating cost per transaction is quite high despite their high daily transaction volume.

SUCCESS FACTORS FOR MICROFINANCE:

1. Information Technology and innovation

Microfinance institutions have long recognised innovation as the key to their success. Chowdhury (2009) argues that the success of the MFI sector in Bangladesh is largely attributable to a significant investment by pioneer MFIs in product innovation and a continuous redesigning of products in accordance with the MFI sector's primary target market, which is the poor segment of society. According to the 2015 RBZ report on the status of the microfinance sector, MFIs must invest in robust Management Information Systems (MIS) to ensure the integrity, relevance, and timeliness of financial data. Currently, the majority of MFIs in Zimbabwe use rudimentary systems that impede the preparation of financial statements that accurately reflect the business's true and fair condition (RBZ., 2015)

2. Staff Training and Motivation

The success of any institution requires that its personnel meet stringent competency requirements. In Asia, staff training and retraining has been identified as the primary factor driving the expansion of MFIs (Chowdhury, 2009). Intellectual capital is widely regarded as a crucial success factor for businesses (Pinz and Helming. 2014; Kamukama et. al, 2010). MFIs must evaluate their recruitment practises in order to attract the most qualified candidates and implement retraining strategies in order to improve their performance (Chirwa et al, 1999; Pinz & Helmont, 2014).

According to Hartungi (2007) and Hulme & Moore (2006), employee incentives contribute significantly to the success of the micro lending industry. The merit-based promotion and bonus system is one of the most frequently used incentive systems in the microfinance industry (Kaplan & Norton, 2009 and Mckin & Hughart, 2005 cited in Chowdhury 2009; Pinz & Helmont, 2014:Hartungi, 2007). Improper compensation of managerial and non-management staff is essential for improved performance.

3. Management and Leadership

Chan (2010) identifies leadership experience and dedication as fundamental MFI success determinants. Management is necessary for the establishment of the MFI's organisational structure, key alliances, and significant networks. In the MFI's oversight arm, it is essential to have a variety of technical expertise.

Researchers have discovered that the degree of autonomy granted by top management is crucial to the success of microfinance institutions (MFIs) (Pinz & Helmont, 2014), Leadership that is dynamic, highly focused, resourceful, and accountable promotes the institution's innovation, growth, success, and viability (Ledgerwood & White, 2006). A solid institutional structure guarantees the separation of management and control.

4. Regulatory Framework

Effective financial intermediation from MFIs requires a favourable and effective regulatory framework, according to Boating and Agyel (2013). Government must eliminate unfair competition to promote the growth of MFIs (Hubka & Zaidi, 2015; Crabb, 2008), as well as ensure the sector's sustainability and maturity (Kimando & Kihoro, 2012). The regulation of lending rates should take into account the viability of MFIS, which in the majority of cases cannot survive under a low interest rate regime because they cannot maintain their costs and business model in an environment where regulators have imposed a rate cap. The primary objective of regulators must be to implement policies and regulations that ensure the prudent operation of MFIs (Kimando & Kihoro, 2012; Servinet al., 2012; Ledgerwood & White, 2006).

Key policy issues should enhance depositor protection by preserving the stability of financial institutions and borrower protection by ensuring that interest rates are affordable (Ledgerwood & White, 2006). MFIs should be governed in a manner that does not exclude small and innovative forms of microfinancing. Regulation should also improve micro credit institution resource mobilisation (Ledgerwood and White, 2006)

5. Prudent Risk Management

Given the high risk exposure of MFIs, particularly to default, effective risk management measures are required. The majority of MFIs are deficient in risk identification, measurement, control, and monitoring (Bounoula & Rihane, 2014; Kimando & Kihori, 2012; RBZ, 2015). To reduce default, proper screening of loan applicants is necessary. Subprime loans always result in unsustainable levels of non-performing loans; therefore, the lending process must be constantly reexamined (Caudil, 2012 as cited in Pinz& Helming, 2014). Asset quality ultimately depends on the institution's selection criteria, so selection is crucial.

6. Coverage, Reach and Marketing

For sustainability, MFIs must have a high financial coverage of the market, which consists primarily of the financially excluded poor and Small to Medium Enterprises (SMEs), as well as a high coverage of products. To reach the entire target (Kimando & Kihoro, 2012: RBZ. 2015), MFIS must offer a variety of tailored financial packages to the market. This will enable MFIs to reach the large numbers required for sustainability. In addition to concentrating on specific small communities, there is a need for a broader geographical coverage and reach. The RBZ report on the status of the microfinance sector (2015) indicates that only a small number of MFIs have branch networks throughout Zimbabwe, resulting in a skewed market structure in which, out of 120 MFIs that submitted returns to the RBZ, 19 hold a loan book greater than one million, accounting for 87.18 percent of the market share. A broader geographic reach may increase the institution's revenue generation and sustainability.

According to Ngumbao (2012), an MFI's success hinges on its marketing strategy. There is a need to examine financial packages and the delivery system in order to better adapt to clients' ever-changing needs and boost customer loyalty. Goal achievement for MFIs requires proper marketing and competitive positioning (Ledgerwood & White, 2006), particularly branding and effectively communicating to consumers the core benefits or value proposition inherent in securing a relationship with the MFL. Researchers emphasise the necessity of matching the MFI's strength with identified market opportunities (Ledgerwood & White, 2006; Ngumban, 2012).

7. Resource Access

Literature reveals that the key to the success of MFIs is the capacity to access resources at an affordable and sustainable cost relative to the portfolio's average yield. The inability of numerous MFIs to access and structure funding (Ledgerwood & White, 2006) has restrained their growth. There are obvious advantages to converting a non-deposit accepting MFI into one that accepts deposits in order to increase the diversification and expansion of existing funding sources. MFIs may need to seek patient capital due to the impact of excessive debt on their return on equity, necessitating the adoption of an optimal capital structure that maximises return on equity and minimises cost of capital (Ledgerwood & White, 2006).

8. Corporate Governance

The corporate governance practises of an organisation have a substantial impact on consumer and business confidence. According to the 2015 RBZ report on the status of the microfinance sector, transparency, accountability, and truthful disclosure of operations are essential to the success of MFIs in Zimbabwe. Sustainable development and growth of MFIs require strong leadership, vision, and skills at the corporate level (Ledgerwood & White, 2006); otherwise, the public may lose faith in MFIs, particularly those that accept public deposits. Many MFIs do not separate ownership and management, which hinders the implementation of proper corporate governance practises. Consensus exists regarding the dependence of MFI performance on the ownership and governance structure, which translates to what Ledger wood and White (2006) refer to as ownership and governance risk, particularly for non-deposit-taking institutions where ownership and control are not separated.

ISSUES OF MICROFINANCE:

1.   The effect of governance mechanism on MFI performance

Boards are essential in microfinance due to the limited influence of external market forces. The board is a mechanism of governance that aids in resolving agency issues between owners and managers. In empirical corporate governance literature, the proportion of outside or independent board directors is used to measure the degree of alignment between the board and shareholder objectives. The board of directors supervises and advises management. There is a correlation between the proportion of the board and firm value, according to empirical research (Hermalin and Weishball, 2003).

There is evidence that female board members devote more time to mentoring (Oster and O'Reagan, 2003). According to a study of the largest Fortune 1000 companies, board diversity influences corporate performance, as corporations with a high proportion of women and ethnic minorities perform better (Carter, Simmons and Simpsons, 2003).

The MFI board has distinctive qualities. It is not unusual for the board to include representation from a number of important stakeholders. Donors, equity investors, insiders (employees and managers), and creditors (who frequently provide a significant amount of funding for micro loans) are the major stakeholders in an MFI. Some MFI boards include individual clients (Campion, 1998). The relative influence of these diverse stakeholders affects outreach and long-term viability (Hartarska, 2004).

The incentives of top management have been cited as a crucial governance mechanism because they ensure management's alignment with shareholder interests (John & Qian, 2004). In other words, it is a mechanism for resolving conflicts of interest between managers and shareholders. Brick et al. (2006) note that even director compensation can impact performance. High-powered incentives may encourage bank managers to take greater risks to achieve the outreach objective, at the expense of the institution's depositors, who would suffer if the bank failed (John & John, 1993).

Regulation could have an effect on the performance of the MFI if it shifts the focus away from outreach and sustainability. In order to promote the safety of the MFI and, more generally, the safety of the financial system, regulators may encourage less risky behaviour on the part of the manager. Less risk taking, however, is equivalent to lower returns, which may affect the preference of those who fund MFIs in the hope that these institutions will serve more risky clients (the poor) and still generate profits, as well as the preferences of others who fund MFIs (Hartarska, 2004).

Auditing is an efficient method of supervision. Internal audit aids in identifying problem areas and preventing major collapse by encouraging independent, objective evaluation of the organization's internal governance structure and operational effectiveness.

Reporting all audit findings accurately and in a timely manner is crucial for assessing the institution's status and the need for any strategy changes (Steinward, 2000).

In the absence of developed equity and debt markets, donors and investors rely on independent evaluations of the MFIs' performance, according to Hartsarka (2004). The microfinance rating reflects a rating agency's assessment of an entity's overall creditworthiness and ability to meet its financial obligations. Unlike conventional rating agencies, which evaluate the riskiness of issued debt, microfinance rating agencies evaluate the MFI's outreach and sustainability.

2. The effect of management information systems on MFI performance

Information systems technology plays a crucial role in microfinance because it enables microfinance institutions to monitor, analyse, and report on their operations and various performance goals, such as outreach and profitability. Such reports are beneficial for administration, donors, and regulators (CGAP, 2005). The growth, expansion, or advancement of microfinance institutions frequently presents numerous monitoring and financial management challenges. According to Okeeffe and Fredrick (2002), a management information system facilitates fundamental changes in an institution through the availability of information without interfering with microfinance operations.

Orr (2000) observes that if there is a single key to business survival in the 1990s and beyond, it is the ability to analyse, plan, and respond to rapidly changing business conditions. For this, top executives require more information than ever before. In the microfinance industry, an institution that develops a system capable of producing accurate, timely, and comprehensive data on its operations, particularly its loan portfolio, will improve its financial performance and increase its client base (Waterfield and Ramsing, 1998).

Methodological issues, staff development, and even funding frequently do not prove to be the most significant growth constraints. Rather, the ability of an institution to track the status of its portfolio in a timely and accurate manner often determines the success or failure of its lending and savings operations, and thus the institution itself (Ledgerwood, 1999).

Ferramd and Havers (1999) explain that information is one of the central problems of microfinance and that its significance is complicated as MFIs scale up with increasing management layers, all of which depend on the correct flow of information to make decisions at their various levels.

Management Information Systems have enabled the expansion and transformation of Microfinance Institutions' operations (Water and Ramsing, 1998). As the number of microfinance clients exceeds a few thousand, microfinance managers lose the ability to maintain personal contact for field-level information, which impacts their portfolio and financial performance (Omasaja, 2007).

Okeeffe and Fredrick (2002) explain that transformation places new demands on the ability of microfinance institutions to centralise data from various operating locations. Due to regulatory reporting requirements and liquidity management, Head Office must be more frequently and accurately informed about the position and performance of their branches.

Waterfield and Ramsing (1998) assert that for a microfinance institution to function efficiently and effectively, the more accurate its data, the more effectively it can manage its resources. This is supported by Ledgerwood (1999), who argues that good management information systems can improve the work of field staff by allowing them to better monitor their portfolios and serve an increasing number of clients. It assists senior management in orchestrating the work of the entire organisation and making well-informed operational and strategic decisions by monitoring the health of microfinance institutions using a set of carefully selected reports and indicators.

According to Mainhart (1999), microfinance is predicated on information. Management Information Systems store vast quantities of vital business data, ranging from basic client information to detailed portfolio analysis statistics. They function as a conduit through which raw data is transformed into useful and actionable information, thereby facilitating the effective management of a microfinance institution.

3. The effect of funding on performance of MFIs

According to Khachatyran (2010), microfinance institutions require financial resources to fulfil their long-term commitments, which makes the role of funding institutions to microfinance very significant. The capital accounts play multiple roles in supporting the daily operations of financial institutions and ensuring their long-term viability. It provides a buffer against the possibility of insolvency by absorbing financial and operating losses until management can address the institution's issues and restore profitability (Rose and Hudgins, 2010).

Smith and Rupp (2002) explain that a company can achieve a sustainable competitive advantage through its scarce financial resources. The availability of funds enables the financial institution to develop new services and facilities, according to Rose and Hudgins (2010). The majority of financial service providers eventually outgrow their initial facilities. A financial firm will be able to expand into larger quarters or build additional outreach offices with the help of additional capital or funds in order to keep up with its expanding market and to follow its customers.

According to Ledgerwood (1999), capital fosters public confidence and reassures creditors regarding an institution's financial stability. Capital also acts as a check on the growth of the financial institution, ensuring that growth is sustainable over time. Lenders whose funds do not grow quickly enough or decline significantly may lose market share in the competition for their larger advancing customers (Rose and Hudgins, 2010).

Reserves are established by a financial institution to absorb losses that have a high probability of occurring and that are distinct from the institution's general business risk. For instance, an increase in interest rates on funds borrowed by the institution without the ability to increase its loan rates proportionally will result in a decrease in profits, all else being equal. The inability of a financial institution to account for changes in interest rates constitutes general business risk (The Accion Camel, 1998).

Despite the success of numerous MFIs, millions of individuals with low incomes in developing nations still lack access to financial services. High operating costs and capital restraints in the MFI industry have prevented MFIs from meeting the immense demand (Bogan, 2008).

References:

introduction and definition. (2012, 5 13). Retrieved from slideshare: https://www.slideshare.net/yogi3250/impact-of-micro-finance-on-living-standard-empowerment-and-poverty-alleviation-of-poor-women-a-case-study-of-north-india

Evolution, features, need, types, challenge, regulatory framework, aim of supportive regulative framework . (n.d.). Retrieved from youtube: https://www.youtube.com/watch?v=VGUL7k7jSlA

CHAPTER XI

Venture Capital And Angel Investors – A Bloodline for Start-Ups

Pallavi Rajai; Gaurav Singh Rajput; Shreha Singh Rathod; Khusboo Shah; Anamika Mishra

1. INTRODUCTION

- Start-ups are new businesses founded to create a one-of-a-kind product or service, bring it to market, and make it irresistible and irreplaceable to customers.
- A start-up, founded on innovation, aims to improve existing products or create entirely new categories of goods and services, disrupting entrenched ways of thinking and doing business for entire industries. (Contributor: Rebecca Baldridge, 2022)

1.1 START-UPS FINANCING

- Start-up financing refers to the initial infusion of funds required to turn an idea (by launching a business) into a reality. Large lenders, such as banks, are not interested in starting a new business.
- The reason for this is that you are not yet at the point where a traditional lender or investor would be interested in you. So one has the option of selling some assets, borrowing against one's home, asking loved ones (family and friends) for loans, and so on.
- However, there are numerous risks involved, including the possibility of bankruptcy and strained relationships with friends and family. This is the difficult part of starting a business: putting so much at risk, but doing so is necessary.
- A good way to achieve success in the field of entrepreneurship is to accelerate initial operations as quickly as possible so that outside investors can see and feel the business venture, as well as understand that a person has taken some risk to get it to that level.
- Some businesses can be bootstrapped as well (attempting to found and build a company from personal finances or from the operating revenues

of the new company). They can be built quickly enough to make money without the assistance of investors who would otherwise come in and dictate the terms.

- A strong business plan is required to successfully launch a business and get it to the point where large investors are interested in putting their money into it. It is also necessary to seek advice from experienced entrepreneurs and experts – people who may invest in the business in the future (ICAI, Final Course, Paper 2, Startup Finance, n.d.)

1.2 TYPES OF START-UP FUNDING

	EQUITY FINANCING	DEBT FINANCING	GRANTS
BRIEF	Equity financing entails selling a portion of a company's equity in exchange for funds.	Debt financing entails borrowing money and repaying it with interest.	A grant is a financial award given to a company by an entity to facilitate a goal or incentivize performance.
NATURE	There is no repayment component for the invested funds.	Invested funds must be repaid with interest within a specified time frame.	There is no repayment component for the invested funds.
RISK	Financer: His investment comes with no guarantees. Start-ups must surrender a portion of their ownership to shareholders.	Financer: The lender has no say in how the business operates. Startups: As collateral, you may be required to provide a business asset.	Financer: There is a risk that the start-up will fail to meet the goal or objective for which the grant was provided. Start-ups: There is a risk that the start-up will not receive a portion of the grant for a variety of reasons.
THRESHOLD OF COMMITMENT	While start-ups face less pressure to meet repayment deadlines, investors are constantly striving to meet growth targets.	Startups must constantly adhere to repayment timelines, which necessitates greater efforts to generate cash flows in order to meet interest repayments.	Grants are distributed in various tranches based on the achievement of the corresponding milestone. As a result, a status is constantly striving to

Source: (Funding Guide , n.d.)

1.3 STAGES OF START-UPS AND SOURCE OF FUNDING

Start-ups can obtain funding from a variety of sources.

The source of funding, however, should typically correspond to the stage of operations of the start-up.

STAGE	MEANING	SOURCES OF FUNDING
Ideation **[Pre-Seed Stage]**	This is the stage at which the entrepreneur has an idea and is working to make it a reality. The amount of money required at this stage is usually small. Furthermore, at the early stages of the startup lifecycle, there are few and mostly informal channels for raising funds.	1. Bootstrapping/Self-financing 2. Business Plan/Pitching Events for Friends and Family
Validation **[Seed Stage]**	A start-up has a prototype ready and needs to validate the potential demand for its product/service at this stage. This is known as a 'Proof of Concept (POC),' and it is followed by the big market launch. A start-up must conduct field trials, test the product on a small number of potential customers, onboard mentors, and form a formal team.	1. Government Loan Programs for Incubators 2. Angel Investors Crowdfunding
Early Traction **[Series A Stage]**	The products or services of a start-up have been launched in the market at the Early Traction stage. At this stage, key performance indicators such as customer base, revenue, app downloads, and so on become important.	1. Funds for Venture Capital 2. Banks and Non-Banking Financial Institutions (NBFCs) 3. Funds for Venture Debt
Scaling **[Series B, C, D & E]**	At this point, the startup is experiencing rapid market growth and rising revenues.	1. Private Equity/Investment Firm Venture Capital Funds
Exit Options	-	1. Mergers and Acquisitions (M&A) 2. Buybacks and Initial Public Offerings (IPOs)Mergers and Acquisitions (M&A) 3. Buybacks and Initial Public Offerings (IPOs)

Source: (Funding Guide , n.d.)

2. ANGEL INVESTORS

Angel investors are wealthy individuals who put their own money into start-up businesses.

Angel investors invest in small start-ups or entrepreneurs.

- Angel investors' capital may be a one-time investment to help the business take off, or it may be a continuous infusion of funds to support and carry the company through its difficult early stages.
- Angel investors offer better terms than other lenders because they typically invest in the entrepreneur starting the business rather than the viability of the business.
- Angel investors are more concerned with assisting start-ups in taking their first steps than with the potential profit from the business.
- Angel investors are the polar opposite of venture capitalists. Informal investors, angel funders, private investors, seed investors, and business angels are all terms for angel investors.
- These are wealthy individuals who provide start-up capital in exchange for ownership equity or convertible debt. Some angel investors use online crowdfunding platforms to invest, while others form angel investor networks to pool capital.
- Unlike venture capitalists, who manage money pooled from many other investors and place it in a strategically managed fund, angel investors typically use their own money. Though angel investors are typically individuals, the entity providing the fund may be a limited liability company, a business, a trust, or an investment fund, among many other options.
- Angel investors who seed start-ups that fail in their early stages lose their entire investment. As a result, professional angel investors seek opportunities with a clear exit strategy, such as acquisitions or initial public offerings (IPOs)(ICAI, Final Course, Paper 2, Startup Finance, n.d.).

2.1. ADVANTAGES OF BRINGING ANGEL INVESTORS

1. **There are no geographical or industry constraints.**

Despite operating in a small town or in a high-risk industry, a start-up can raise millions of dollars from an angel investor. While angel investors do accept private equity, they do not intervene in the operations of the company unless required or requested.

1. **There is very little paperwork.**

While you will need to prepare a pitch, financial projections, and a business plan, you will not need as much paperwork to close an angel investment as you would a business loan.

3. **Guidance and assistance are provided.**

You are not only receiving funding from an angel investor, but you are also learning from them. This is important for a startup because you can rely on the investor's expertise when making business decisions, leading to greater success.

4. **There are networking opportunities available.**

Angel investors can connect you with potential clients, which can help your business grow. Investors can also connect you with other start-ups they have supported, which can aid in the formation of strategic alliances.

5. **Future funding assistance is available.**

Because angel investors are repaid when your company receives future funding rounds, there is an incentive for investors to assist your company in reaching that point as soon as possible. Angel investors will network with other investors to help speed up the process, giving you more time to focus on running your business rather than looking for future investors.

6. **There is no need for collateral, i.e. personal assets.**

Because angel funding is not a loan, it does not require collateral and does not require instalment payments, allowing them to invest all of the capital into a company.

2.2. DISADVANTAGES OF BRINGING ANGEL INVESTORS

1. **Availability is based on who you know**

If you rely on unknown angel investors, your chances of convincing one of them to invest in your company are significantly lower.

2. **Average amounts are less than venture capital**

Because the amount of capital required may be less than the actual need for the business, you may need to proceed with another round of funding soon after receiving angel investment.

3. **Giving up a share of your business**

Angel investors typically receive a 20% premium on convertible debt. Investors can convert debt to equity at the next valuation. The more funds you raise, the more equity you give away in your business. Due to the equity given away in angel investments, original owners may become minority owners in some cases. (Financing > Pros and Cons of Using Angel Investors to Fund Your Business, 2022)

2.3. CHOOSING THE RIGHT ANGEL

- An investment transaction is a two-way street.
- Finding someone who understands your market and can relate to your business proposition is essential.
- How?
- Examine their references thoroughly.
- Check to see if they have already invested in one of your competitors.
- Could you collaborate with them? Personality clashes can be a source of contention.
- Examine their previous investments to see if they were a success or a failure.
- Is their planned level of business involvement appropriate for you?
- Do they have a track record of sticking with companies through thick and thin?
- Do they have useful contacts for potential business partners and investors? (Mahzan Sulaiman, n.d.)

2.4. LISTING FEW ACTIVE ANGEL INVESTORS IN INDIA

1. Ritesh Agarwal
2. Kunal Bahl and Rohit Bansal
3. Kunal Shah
4. Binny Bansal
5. Anupam Mittal

3. VENTURE CAPITAL

- Venture Capital Fund refers to an investment vehicle that manages funds from investors looking to invest in start-ups and small businesses with high growth potential.
- Professionals who invest alongside management in young, rapidly growing companies with the potential to become significant economic contributors provide venture capital.

Venture Capitalists generally

- Finance new and rapidly growing companies
- Purchase equity securities
- Assist in the development of new products or services
- Add value to the company through active participation.

3.1 CHARACTERISTICS OF VENTURE CAPITAL FINANCING:

(i) Long time horizon: The fund would invest over a long period of time. The minimum investment period is three years, and the maximum period is ten years.

(ii) Lack of liquidity: When Venture Capitalists invest, they consider the liquidity factor. It expects less liquidity on the equity it receives and, as a result, will invest in that format. They weigh the liquidity premium in relation to the price and required return.

(iii) High Risk: Venture capitalists are not afraid to take risks. It operates on the high risk/high return principle. As a result, high risk does not rule out venture capital as an investment option.

(iv) Equity Participation: Most of the time, Venture Capitalists will invest in the form of a company's equity. This would allow Venture Capitalists to participate in management and assist the company's growth. Furthermore, if a VC participates in a company's equity, they can oversee many board decisions.

3.2. ADVANTAGES OF BRINGING VENTURE CAPITAL IN THE COMPANY:

1. It provides long-term equity financing, establishing a solid capital base for future growth.
2. The venture capitalist is a business partner with whom you share both the risks and the rewards.
3. Business success and capital gain are rewarded for venture capitalists.
4. Based on previous experience with other companies in similar situations, the venture capitalist can provide practical advice and assistance to the company.
5. The venture capitalist also has a network of contacts in a variety of fields that can help the company.
6. If additional rounds of funding are required to finance growth, the venture capitalist may be able to provide them.
7. Venture capitalists have extensive experience preparing companies for an Initial Public Offering (IPO) of their shares on stock exchanges or overseas stock exchanges such as NASDAQ (ICAI,Final Course, Paper 2, Startup Finance. , n.d.).

3.3. DISADVANTAGES OF BRINGING VENTURE CAPITAL IN THE COMPANY :

1. The founder's ownership stake is being reduced.
2. Create a conflict of interest.
3. It can take time to receive approval.
4. There must be a formal reporting structure and a board of directors.
5. Obtaining Venture Capital can be difficult.
6. Finding investors can divert founders' attention away from their core business.
7. The overall cost of financing can be high.

For example, two start-ups each require $1 million and are worth $10 million. The first company obtains a 10-year Small Business Administration (SBA) loan at 10% interest, while the second raises $1 million for 10% equity. If both companies sell for $100 million in ten years, the first *company's founders paid $600,000 in interest for the loan and retained full equity, while the second company gave up $10 million in sale proceeds due to equity dilution (Thunstrom, 2022), (Personal Finance > Venture Capital , n.d.).*

4. VENTURE CAPITALISTS' INVESTMENT PROCESS

The entire Venture Capital Investment process can be segregated into the following steps:

1. Deal Origination:

- Venture capitalists work either directly or indirectly. Many practising Chartered Accountants would primarily act as intermediaries, and Venture Capitalists would obtain the deal through them.
- Before sourcing the deal, Venture Capitalists would inform the intermediary or its employees of the following information so that the sourcing entity does not waste time:

  - Sector focus
  - Stages of business focus
  - Promoter focus
  - Turn over focus

- The company would present a detailed business plan that included a business model, financial plan, and exit strategy.
- All of these aspects are addressed in a document known as an Investment Memorandum (IM). The IM also performs a preliminary valuation.

2. Screening:

Once the case has passed due diligence, it will proceed to deal structuring. The agreement is written in such a way that both parties benefit. The convertible structure is frequently used to ensure that the promoter retains the right to buy back the share. Furthermore, in many structures, the Venture Capitalists may require the promoter to sell a portion of its stake alongside the Venture Capitalists in order to facilitate the exit. This type of clause is known as a tag-along clause.The deal will be sent to Venture Capitalists for review once it has been sourced. A committee of senior level Venture Capitalists typically conducts the screening. Following the screening, the company would be selected for further consideration.

3. Due Diligence:

- The screening decision would be made using the information supplied by the company. Once the decision to proceed is made, the Venture Capitalists will conduct due diligence.
- This is primarily the process by which Venture Capitalists attempt to verify the authenticity of the documents obtained. External bodies, primarily renowned consultants, are typically in charge of this.
- Due diligence fees are typically paid by Venture Capitalists. However, depending on the veracity of the document agreement, this can be shared between the investor (Venture Capitalists) and the Investee (the company) in many cases.

4. Deal Structuring:

Once the case has passed due diligence, it will proceed to deal structuring. The agreement is written in such a way that both parties benefit. The convertible structure is frequently used to ensure that the promoter retains the right to buy back the share. Furthermore, in many structures, the Venture Capitalists may require the promoter to sell a portion of its stake alongside the Venture Capitalists in order to facilitate the exit. This type of clause is known as a tag-along clause.

5. Post Investment Activity:

The Venture Capitalists nominate their nominee for the company's board of directors in this section. The company must follow certain guidelines such as strong MIS, a strong budgeting system, strong corporate governance, and other Venture Capitalist covenants, as well as keep the Venture Capitalists updated on certain milestones on a regular basis. If a milestone is not met, the company must explain why to Venture Capitalists. Furthermore, Venture Capitalists would ensure that professional management is established in the company.

6. Exit plan:

- When investing, Venture Capitalists would ask the promoter or company to detail the exit strategy. Exit occurs primarily in two ways:
- 'Sell to third party(ies)' is one option. This sale could take the form of an initial public offering (IPO) or a private placement to other venture

capitalists.

- The second method of exit is for the promoter to make a buy-back commitment at a predetermined rate (generally between IRR of 18 percent to 25 percent). If the exit does not take the form of an IPO or a third-party sale, the promoter will buy back. In many transactions, the promoter buyback method is used, which means that the promoter has the first right of buyback.. (ICAI,Final Course, Paper 2, Startup Finance. , n.d.)

MOST ACTIVE VENTURE CAPITAL FIRMS FOR INDIAN START-UPS IN H1 2022

1. Better Capital
2. Sequoia Capital India
3. Titan Capital
4. Tiger Global
5. Trifecta Capital

Figure 1: Top Investors backing startups in India

(Source: Inc. 42)

5. DIFFERENCES BETWEEN ANGEL INVESTORS AND VENTURE CAPITAL

Criteria	Angel Investment	Venture Capital
Meaning	Individual investors make angel investments in pre-revenue businesses.	A company that pools money from individuals and institutions usually invests in the pre-profitability business.
Risk Level	Because the revenue stream is uncertain, this investment is extremely risky.	This investment is less risky because the revenue stream is proven, but the profitability of the invested company is not yet visible.
Investment size	The investment size is limited to a few million dollars.	Because of the pooling of funds, investment sizes can range from a few million to tens of millions because a venture capitalist has access to a much larger pool of funds.
Type of investment	The investment is made through Equity and SAFE (simple agreement for future equity), in which the invested business grants the angel investor the right to purchase shares in future equity offerings.	The investment is made with equity and/or convertible debt.
Time for investment decision and sales pitch	Because this investment involves a single investor, the decision-making process is sped up.	Venture capitalists take longer to make investment decisions because they must address multiple stakeholders with competing interests. As a result, convincing the venture capitalist to make an investment decision is more difficult.
Money	Use their own money to make investment.	To make an investment, money is pooled from insurance companies, funds, foundations, and corporations.

6. CURRENT SCENARIO OF START-UPS

Figure 2: Current scenario of start-ups India:

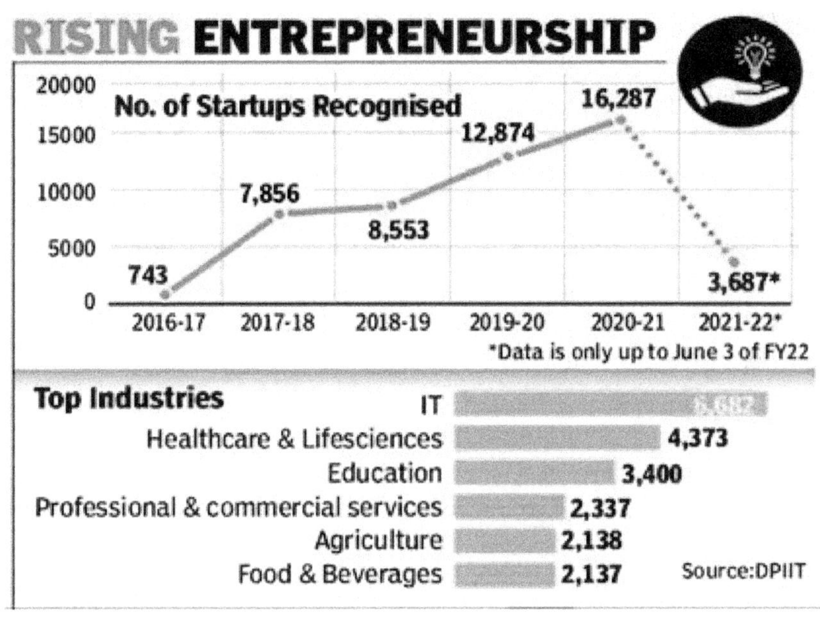

Source: DPIIT

THE STATE OF THE INDIAN STARTUP ECONOMY

Figure 3: The state of the Indian Startup Economy

Source: Inc42 The State of Indian Start-up Economy Report, 2022

References:

(n.d.). Retrieved from Mahzan Sulaiman: https://www.mahzansulaiman.com/single-post/who-are-angel-investors-the-disadvantages-advantages

Financing > Pros and Cons of Using Angel Investors to Fund Your Business. (2022, 1 31). Retrieved from FitSmallBusiness: https://fitsmallbusiness.com/angel-investors-pros-cons/

Funding Guide . (n.d.). Retrieved from startupindia: https://www.startupindia.gov.in/content/sih/en/funding.html

ICAI,Final Course, Paper 2, Startup Finance. . (n.d.). Retrieved from The Institute of Chartered Accountants of India: https://resource.cdn.icai.org/67852bos54415-cp14.pdf

Personal Finance > Venture Capital . (n.d.). Retrieved from Groww: https://groww.in/p/venture-capital

Rebecca Baldridge(Contributor), B. C. (2022, 10 16). *Advisor>Business.* Retrieved from Forbes : https://www.forbes.com/advisor/business/what-is-a-startup/

Thunstrom, T. (2022, 01 31). *Financing>20 Venture Capital Advantages and Disadvantages.* Retrieved from FitSmallBusiness: https://fitsmallbusiness.com/venture-capital-advantages-and-disadvantages/

CHAPTER XII

Biases in Behavioral Finance

Ms. Bina Patel; Ms. Anjali Singh; Ms. Mitali Suthar; Ms. Khushbu Thummar;
Ms. Ritu Verma; Ms. Drashti Vora

1. INTRODUCTION

Behavioral finance is the study of cerebral influences on investors and fiscal requests. At its core, behavioral finance is about relating and explaining inefficiency and mispricing in fiscal requests. It uses trials and exploration to demonstrate that humans and fiscal requests aren't always rational, and the opinions they make are frequently flawed. However, behavioral finance offers answers and explanations If you're wondering how feelings and impulses drive share prices.

1. TYPES OF BIASES IN BEHAVIORAL FINANCE

There are majorly five types of bias, which are:

1. Heuristic Behavior

Understanding behavioural finance allows finance directors to make better decisions. Traditional finance Is guided by investors' rational decisions, whereas ultramodern finance considers both cognitive and emotional visions in investment decisions- timber. In an uncertain and changing environment, investors form opinions based on trial and error or old rules of thumb. However, cognitive and emotional factors are included when evaluating investment volition, which can exclude rational gest in the decision-making process (Puaschunder, Julia, & Nudgitize, March 10, 2017).

2. Representativeness

Decisions are based on the outcomes of the most recent investment; if the investor's decisions in the previous investment resulted in success, the investor will continue to make the same choices in the next investment without taking into account the various uncertainty patterns. This is similar to making assumptions based on recent experience. Investors try to buy hot or good stocks rather than bad performance stocks, demonstrating representative bias in which investors overreact.

3. Overconfidence

Confidence is generally the auspicious gesture of an investor that courage his in the investment, but overconfidence is effective in contradiction of confidence because in overconfidence substantially investors ignore the threat and Query element due to preliminary continue the success and made further trading, so the probability of failure increased.

4. Randomness

The perception of fate and superstitions by mortals can inform investment decisions. Some people have a superstitious belief in luck, and as a result, their decisions are based on veritably low levels of rationality, as they believe that events are predetermined by luck. Some people, however, have strong inner control; they disregard fate and superstitions, and their opinions are based on rationality factors, as they recognise that their opinions are the responsibility of issues.

5. Confirmation Bias

Evidence bias is the tendency of humans to diligently seek information that supports their predetermined beliefs. Individuals pay a disproportionate amount of attention to information that confirms their beliefs. In addition, they tend to disregard any information that contradicts their beliefs. It must be understood that the investor is not acting intentionally. Instead, the entire process occurs unconsciously. Investors frequently hold beliefs that are not the result of diligent effort. The investor's mind seeks out information that confirms his or her beliefs while ignoring information that contradicts them. The issue with evidence bias is that the investor believes they have conducted the necessary due diligence when they have not. A customer whose effects are concentrated in a particular sector or group of stocks, for instance, may only absorb positive news and disregard negative news regarding these investments.

6. Recency Bias

Recency bias is the phenomenon in which we give more weight to recent events than to those that occurred in the past. We base our decisions on recent occurrences, anticipating that they will continue into the future. This can result in erroneous decisions, such as selling high-return investments during a market downturn.

As an illustration: Suppose that the investment's market value increased to $130,000 over the past four years, only to decrease to $121,000 in the most recent month. Here, the investor views his investment performance as a loss of $10,000 in one month, rather than a total gain of $20,000 over four years. Thus, this is merely a case of recency bias (Joseph, 2016).

Ways to overcome recency bias are as follows:

- Better understanding the markets requires recognising that a stock market is a place where the market operates in cycles. It is important to understand and observe their timings up to a certain point during this period of ups and downs. Investing in assets with stellar performance will increase returns.
- Clarify your financial objectives: all plans must include short-, medium-, and long-term objectives. Planning enables investors to invest their money in a superior investment. As investments are risky because they offer both high profits and losses, building a strong portfolio includes managing some assets in low-risk debt funds as well. This will increase confidence and prevent panic by reducing the influence of recency bias.
- Employ financial consultants: As it is human nature to be susceptible to recency bias, it is essential to hire a consultant or advisor with market expertise and experience.

7. Herd Mentality

Herd bias is the tendency of individuals to imitate the behaviour of a large group regardless of whether or not they would make the same decision collectively. The lack of differentiation in decision-making causes investors to imitate the decisions of other investors without considering the consequences of technical and introductory examination of specialists in the field. Herding could be considered the opposite of overconfidence regarding the effectiveness of information. Examples of human-based herd behaviour include voting, demonstrations, general strikes, sporting events, religious gatherings, and everyday decision-making, judgement, and opinion formation (Muhammad, Muhammad , & Muhammad , 2020).

8. Familiarity Bias

Due to investment barriers, transaction costs, and other asymmetries in information, investors prefer to invest in domestic securities over foreign securities. Thus, investor decision-making is also influenced by home bias. The fluctuation of stock prices in response to rational and illogical events stimulates decision makers to form optimistic or pessimistic opinions. When the psychology heuristic tendency is implemented in the Fiscal Request, it regulates which investors bear an over/under response. This rebuke of psychology in stock prices demonstrates the influence of behavioural finance on decision-making. Familiarity bias refers to the tendency to select fewer investments that you perceive to be within your area of expertise. For instance, you may feel secure purchasing shares of a company for which you work, or you may feel at ease investing in a field related to your profession. To overcome this bias, you must diversify your portfolio and increase its size to lower your level of risk (De, Giorgio, & Bruno, 1997) (Coval, 1999).

3. CONCLUSION

Behavioral finance enables us to comprehend how financial judgments regarding effects such as investments, payments, threats, and specific debt are significantly influenced by human emotion, impulses, and cognitive limitations in processing and responding to information. The framework of behavioural finance encompasses a variety of decision-maker actions. In addition to passions, moods, and ecological factors, which are also incorporated into investment decision-making, the structure of the proposition excerpts another variable that influences investment opinions. As a result of behavioural impulses, individuals do not necessarily act rationally and consider all available information during the decision-making process. Over the past three decades, behavioural finance has successfully integrated psychology into finance in order to comprehend the emotional state of investors and their financial requests.

Top of Form

References:

Coval, J. D. (1999). Home Bias at Home. *Journal of Finance 54 (6), 2045 -2073* , 2045 -2073.

De, S., Giorgio, & Bruno, G. (1997). International Investment Pricing and Portfolio Diversification with Familiarity Bias Risk. *Journal of Finance* , 1881-1912.

Joseph, D. (2016). Behavioural Finance: An Introspection of investors Psychology. *Indian Commerce and Management Studies, 1 (1)* .

Muhammad, A. S., Muhammad , T., & Muhammad , F. S. (2020). Behavioural Finance Biases in Investment Decision Making. *International Journal of Accounting, Finance and Risk Mamangement* , 5, 69-75.

Puaschunder, Julia, M., & Nudgitize, M. (March 10, 2017). A Behavioura Finance Approach to Minimize Losses and Maximize Profits from Heuristics and Biases. *International Journal of Management Excellence,10,2,* , 1241-1256.

CHAPTER XIII

FDI & FII (Comparison & Contrast Analysis)

Ms. Anjali Tiwari; Mr. Kaivan Madrasi; Ms. Jill Patel; Mr. Darshit Patwa; Ms. Muskan Salecha

1. INTRODUCTION:

Foreign direct investment (FDI) and foreign institutional investment (FII) have played a significant role in the development of numerous economies. Moreover, among the various forms of foreign assistance, many developing nations view foreign direct investment (FDI) and foreign institutional investment (FII) as an important component of their development strategy.

The Foreign direct investment (FDI) and foreign institutional investment (FII) flows are usuallypreferred over the other form of external finance, because they are not debt creating, nonvolatileinnature and their returns depend upon the projects financed by the investor.

Foreign direct investment (FDI) and foreign institutional investment (FII) would also facilitate international trade and knowledge, skill, and technology transfer. Foreign direct investment (FDI) and foreign institutional investment (FII) are the processes by which a resident of one country (the source country) acquires ownership of assets in order to control the production, distribution, and other productive activities of a company in another country.

Since a decade ago, robust economic growth has replaced basic tenets such as self-sufficiency, domestic savings, and infrastructure development. Cross-border trade vanished and paved the way for international business. As the world's most populous nation, India faces many obstacles to economic growth, including societal and financial factors. Trade deficit, interest rates, and inflation are included. Through their investments in the financial system, western nations influenced the economy of India. Thus, foreign capital sources such as FDI and FII have become both dominant and risky players in capital formation. Through direct participation in production areas or investment in stock exchanges, these investments were welcomed. Recent RBI statistics reveal that the majority of capital sources originate from foreign countries. This would affect the financial system and the economy as a whole.

2. CONCEPTUAL FRAMEWORK -INDIAN & GLOBAL TRENDS:

2.1 Definition of FDI:

Foreign Direct Investment, abbreviated as FDI, is an investment in which foreign funds are invested in a company based in a country other than that of the investor. Typically, the investment is made to acquire a long-term stake in the investee company. It is referred to as a direct investment because the investor company seeks significant influence or management control over the foreign company.

Foreign direct investment is regarded as one of the primary means of acquiring external aid. Developed countries with a strong financial standing can provide financing to developing nations with limited financial resources. A foreign investor can acquire controlling ownership through a merger or acquisition, the purchase of shares, participation in a joint venture, or the establishment of a wholly-owned subsidiary.

2.2 Definition of FII:

FII is an abbreviation for Foreign Institutional Investor, which refers to investors who pool their funds to invest in the foreign country's assets. It is a tool for making investors money quickly. Institutional investors are corporations that invest capital in the financial markets of a foreign nation. Before making the investment, it must register with the securities exchange board of the respective country. It consists of banks, mutual funds, insurance firms, hedge funds, etc.

FII plays a crucial role in the economy of any nation. When a foreign company invests or purchases securities, the market trend rises, and when it withdraws its investment, the market trend falls.

2.3 FDI in Indian and Global Context: Recent Trends, Challenges and Way Forward:

Foreign direct investment's (FDI) contribution to economic growth is multidimensional and widely acknowledged in both developed and developing nations. FDI also plays a crucial role in facilitating the international integration of global value chains. However, the flow of FDI is not automatic; it is contingent on a number of factors, including regulatory policy, investment environment, competitiveness, market size, and political stability in the host nation. The shift in the global economy's centre of gravity and a very aggressive policy stance to attract foreign direct investment (FDI) by key countries in the Asian region have resulted in a diversion of FDI towards Asia, particularly to major economies such as China and India. As the majority of Western economies struggled to cope with the COVID-19 pandemic in 2020, the shift in global FDI flows towards Asia accelerated.

According to the 'Investment Trend Monitor' published by the United Nations Conference on Trade and Development (UNCTAD) in January 2021, the COVID-19 pandemic precipitated a sharp decline in global FDI in 2020. In 2020, global FDI plummeted by 42%, falling from approximately $1.5 trillion in 2019 to an estimated $859 billion in 2020. India and China were the only major FDI destination economies to attract growth in FDI flows over the prior year. While FDI flows to India rose by 13 percent to an estimated $57 billion, FDI flows to China rose by 4 percent to an estimated $164 billion. However, FDI inflows to the majority of other major economies, including the United States, Germany, France, the United Kingdom, and Brazil, have declined sharply.

The United States has been the top recipient of foreign direct investment (FDI) flows in the world for decades, but a sharp decline of over 49 percent in 2020 has pushed the country to the second spot, while China, which has long ranked second, has replaced the United States as the top recipient of FDI flows in 2020. Despite the fact that the gap between the United States and China in terms of FDI inflow has been narrowing over the past five years, the United States' fall from the top spot in 2020 is primarily attributable to its handling of the COVID-19 pandemic. However, once the pandemic is contained and pre-pandemic economic growth is restored, the United States will likely regain its position, at least for the next few years. According to the IMF's January 2021 World Economic Outlook Update, the US economy is projected to expand by 5.1% in 2021 and 2.5% in 2022.

Figure 1: Share (%) of India and other major economies in global FDI flows

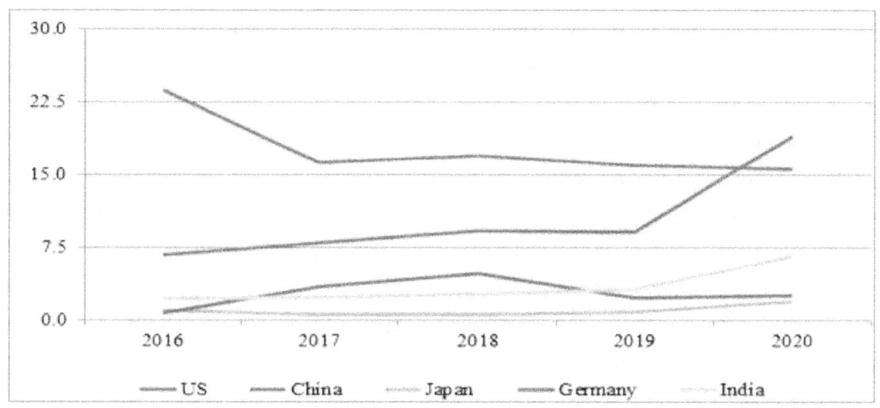

Source: World Investment Report 2020 and UNCTAD's Investment Trend Monitor, January 2021

Note: Data on FDI flows for 2020 are estimated

Figure 1 depicts the fluctuating proportions of the five largest economies in global FDI flows over the past five years. While the United States' share of global FDI flows has steadily decreased from 24 percent in 2016 to 16 percent in 2020, India's and China's share has increased from 2.2 percent and 6.7 percent to 6.6 percent and 19 percent respectively over the same time period. However, it is important to note that the gap between India and China remains notably wide. Since 2017, Japan's FDI share has increased steadily, while FDI flows to Germany have fluctuated. While FDI flows to Japan have consistently been lower than those to India over the past five years, FDI flows to Germany have also been lower than those to India over the past two years.

2.4 FII in Indian and Global Context: Recent Trends, Challenges and Way Forward:

Foreign Institutional Investors (FIIs), also known as Foreign Portfolio Investors (FPIs), constitute a significant category of investors in the Indian capital markets. Almost 20% of the total market capitalization is held by FIIs (as of Jan 2021). Foreign investors view their investments in India as a component of their overall Emerging Market (EM) portfolio. Emerging Markets are typically developing nations with rapid economic growth. Due to the nature of their mature economies, the growth rates of developed economies are typically subdued. FIIs seek higher returns on their investments in EMs, which they obtain. Emerging market economies include the BRIC countries - Brazil, Russia, India, and China.

FII investment trends are influenced by a number of variables, but primarily by:

- The worldwide economy,
- The economic outlook of the institutional investor's home country and the economic outlook of the investment's target market.

By June 2022, FII ownership of the BSE500 index had declined from near-record highs of 21.5% in December 2020 to a decade low of 18.4%. Why has this percentage significantly decreased? Noting that the United States is home to the majority of FIIs that invest in India, the following factors explain why.

Current global geopolitical issues caused by the Russia-Ukraine war have triggered a gas and grain supply crisis. Inflation caused by the war and excess liquidity brought on by the Covid-19 pandemic have prompted Western central banks to take a tough stance on rate hikes.

The United States and western economies are wracked by high inflation. The consumer price index (a measure of inflation) in the United States has reached its highest level since 1981, at 9.1. Recently, Fed Chairman Jerome Powell made it clear that the Fed will continue to aggressively raise interest rates to combat inflation.

Despite crude reaching $120/barrel, India has managed to mitigate the effects of high inflation. According to data released by the government, the GDP for the first quarter of fiscal year 2023 was a promising 13.5%. The economic recovery appears robust in the services and manufacturing sectors.

Investors are more concerned with commodity prices and interest rates than with the conclusion of the Ukraine-Russia conflict. Nevertheless, we are obviously not out of the woods. The Russia-Ukraine conflict has not ended and may even deteriorate. While Fed interest rates are now factored in, the expectation that rate hikes will moderate may not materialise as inflation remains elevated and negative surprises can have global repercussions. Numerous Western analysts anticipate that equity returns in the majority of major economies will be subdued until early 2023. In light of these conditions, the net FII inflows for this calendar year may continue to be negative, although the trend appears to be reversing.

Since FIIs are such a dominant force on the markets, their investments and withdrawals have a significant effect on the markets. A sell-off by FIIs can actually initiate a market correction. However, this trend has changed in India, particularly after the pandemic. Participation by the general public in the markets has increased significantly. In FY 2021 alone, close to 1.4 crore new DEMAT accounts were opened. The retail participation in SIPs through mutual funds, ULIPs, Hybrid funds, and Balanced funds totals between $14 and $15 billion annually. These inflows serve as a buffer against any significant FII selling.

Despite the gloomy global outlook, India's growth fundamentals are superior to those of other EMs. The domestic economy of India has demonstrated strength and resilience. Due to the realignment of global supply chains and a number of other reforms and initiatives, India's long-term outlook has not only remained intact since Covid and Ukraine, but has also grown stronger. This bodes well for the Indian economy over the long term, and investors and analysts are optimistic about its future. FIIs have also realised that India will be the growth engine for the remainder of this year's global economy. Consequently, we could anticipate continued FII inflows in the near future.

3. Advantages and Disadvantages:

3.1 Benefits of Foreign Direct Investment:

Foreign direct investment provides benefits for both the investor and the host nation. These incentives encourage both parties to accept and participate in FDI.

Listed below are several advantages for businesses:

- Market diversification
- Tax incentives
- Lower labour costs
- Preferential tariffs
- Subsidies

The following are some of the benefits for the host country:

- Economic stimulation
- Development of human capital
- Increase in employment
- Exchange rate stability
- Access to management expertise, skills, and technology

The majority of these advantages are based on cost reduction and risk mitigation for businesses. The benefits for host countries are primarily economic.

3.2 Disadvantages of Foreign Direct Investment:

Despite its many advantages, FDI has two major disadvantages, including:

- The entry of large corporations, such as Walmart, may result in the displacement of local businesses. Frequently, Walmart is criticised for driving out local businesses that cannot compete with its low prices.
- Profit repatriation: The primary concern regarding profit repatriation is that firms will not reinvest profits in the host country. This results in significant capital outflows from the host nation.

3.3 Trigger points for FDI to invest in the Indian market:

Sector/activity	Sectorial cap	Entry route
Defence	100%	Automatic up to 74% Government route beyond 74% wherever it is likely to result in access to modern technology or for other reasons to be recorded
Terrestrial broadcasting FM	49%	Government route
Up-linking/down-linking of news and current affairs channels	49%	Government route
Print media	26%	Government route
Publication of Indian editions of foreign magazines dealing with news and current affairs	26%	Government route
Multi-brand retail trading	51%	Government route
Pharmaceuticals (brownfield)	100%	Automatic route up to 74% Government route beyond 74%
Banking - private sector	74%	Automatic route up to 49% Government route beyond 49%
Banking - public sector	20%	Government route
Private security agencies	74%	Automatic route up to 49% Government route beyond 49% and up to 74%
Scheduled air transport services	100%	Automatic route up to 49% (up to 100% for non-resident Indians) Government route beyond 49%

1. Under the FDI policy, FDI is prohibited in:

- the lottery sector;
- gambling and betting;
- Nidhi companies, which borrow and lend money between members;

- trading in transferable development rights;
- real estate and the construction of farmhouses, except for the development of townships, residential or commercial premises, roads or bridges and real estate investment trusts;
- the manufacturing of cigars, cheroots, cigarillos and cigarettes, or tobacco or of tobacco substitutes; and
- activities or sectors not open to private sector investment such as atomic energy and railway operations

3.5 Eligible Securities for FII to Invest in Indian Securities market:

- Securities in the primary and secondary markets, including shares, debentures, and warrants of unlisted, soon-to-be-listed, or publicly traded companies.
- Units of schemes floated by domestic mutual funds, including Unit Trust of India, regardless of whether they are listed on a recognised stock exchange, and units of schemes floated by a Collective Investment Scheme.
- Government Securities Derivatives, such as futures and options, that are traded on a recognised stock exchange. On August 31, 2009, the National Stock Exchange (NSE) debuted interest rate futures, which FIIs can now invest in.
- Security receipts on commercial paper

3.6 Legal limitations of Foreign Institutional Investments:

Generally, FIIs are restricted to investing no more than 24 percent of the paid-in capital of the Indian company receiving the investment. However, FIIs can invest more than 24 percent if the board of directors of the company approves and a special resolution is passed. The investment cap for FIIs in Indian public-sector banks is only 20% of the banks' paid-in capital. Although the 24 percent limit may be increased to 30 percent in the case of specific companies that have obtained shareholder approval for the same amount but not more, the limit cannot exceed 30 percent.

Any FII or sub-account of a FII is permitted to invest up to 10 percent of a company's equity, subject to a total limit of 24 percent for all FIIs, NRIs, and OCBs.

Foreign institutional investors are permitted to invest a maximum amount in debt securities on their account and sub-account, subject to conditions imposed by SEBI. These conditions may be obligatory. Investing in securities issued by asset reconstruction companies or companies subject to the 2002 Security and Reconstruction of Financial Assets and Enforcement of Security Interest Act. The Reserve Bank of India monitors compliance with these limits on a daily basis by instituting cutoff points 2% below the maximum investment amount. This gives it the opportunity to warn the Indian firm receiving the investment before allowing the final 2 percent to be acquired.

4. Latest Development and Trends of FDI and FII In India:

1. **Why are FIIs withdrawing Money from Indian Equities?**

- The Russia Ukraine war:

The Russia-Ukraine conflict dominated the news during the last week of February. uncertainties and geopolitical complexities that arose due to this war have created a fear among foreign investors. This has led to the outflow of FIIs from India.

- High crude oil price:

India is the third largest consumer and importer of crude oil in the world. As crude oil prices increase, the Russia-Ukraine conflict has had a significant impact on the global economy.

- **Changes in the US economy:**

US benchmarks reached record highs, and rising inflation globally has led to an increase in interest rates and a rise in bond yields in the United States and other developed markets.

- Expensive Indian market:

According to stock exchange data, the Sensex reached a price-to-earnings (p/e) ratio of 31 times in October, while the nifty reached a p/e ratio of 28.17 times.

- Depreciation of rupee against US Doller and some other currencies.

4.2 Why are FIIs investments expected to rise soon?

- **Rise in exports:**

Exports and the Indian economy go hand in hand. An increase in India's exports will eventually contribute to the expansion of the economy. When FIIs observe this positive growth in the Indian economy, they become increasingly attracted to it and consequently increase their investments.

- **Strong gap projections:**

The GDP projections assist policymakers and the central bank in determining whether the economy is contracting or expanding, allowing them to take appropriate action. Real GDP growth for the first quarter of fiscal year 2022-23 in India is anticipated to be 17.2 percent, 7 percent, 4.3 percent, and 4.5 percent, respectively.The GDP projections assist policymakers and the central bank in determining whether the economy is contracting or expanding, allowing them to take appropriate action. Real GDP growth for the first quarter of fiscal year 2022-23 in India is anticipated to be 17.2 percent, 7 percent, 4.3 percent, and 4.5 percent, respectively in Q1, Q2, Q3 and Q4.

- **Positive government reforms:**

The Indian government has taken numerous steps to improve the country's economy and FII investments. In addition, business-friendly policies and initiatives such as ease of doing business, make in India, digitalization, and the announcement of production linked incentive (PLI) for various industries such as domestic solar cell and module manufacturing, bulk drug manufacturing, and advanced chemistry cell manufacturing have been implemented.

4.3 853 FDI proposal disposed of in 5 years through FIFP:

In the past five years, 853 foreign direct investment proposals have been processed through the foreign investment facilitation portal. After the foreign investment promotion board was abolished in May 2017, the foreign investment facilitation portal (FIFP) was created.

4.4 FDI inflow hits all-time high of USD 83.57 billion in F.Y.2021-22:

In F.Y. 2021-22, approximately USD 21.34 billion in FDI equity inflows will flow into manufacturing sectors, a 76 percent increase compared to F.Y. 2020-21's USD 12.09 billion.

Computer software & hardware (24.60 percent), services sector (banking, insurance, non-finance/business, outsourcing, R& D courier, tech. testing and analysis, and other) (12.13 percent), automobile industry (11.89 percent), trading (7.72 percent), and construction (infrastructure) activities (7.72 percent) will receive the highest FDI equity inflows during FY 2021-22. (5.52 percent).

4.5 The government has capped 20% FDI limit in LIC under the automatic route:

The insurance amendment bill 2021 was passed on 22 March 2021 to increase the foreign direct investment (FDI) limit in the insurance sector from 49 percent to 74 percent in an effort to attract more foreign insurance players to India.

India permits up to 74 percent foreign direct investment (FDI) in the insurance industry, but this does not apply to LIC, which is governed by the LIC act. Due to its listing, the government may now permit up to 20 percent foreign investment in the insurer.

4.6 Rs. 494 crore FDI received in defence sector since revising policy:

The government has increased the foreign direct investment (FDI) limit from 49 percent to 74 percent under the automatic route and up to 100 percent through the government route in the defence sector, in accordance with the FDI policy effective as of 15 October 2020.

4.7 lava in advanced talks with China's huaqin (the world's largest original design manufacturer for mobile and tablets) to form a joint venture:

The joint venture may be the first of its kind between an Indian company and a Chinese company as a result of the new FDI policy, which permits Chinese companies to enter India after passing the government's rote filter.

4.8 apple will be diversifying its production out of China and begin manufacturing iPhone 14 in India:

Due to the sudden covid-19 lockdown at the key iPhone pro manufacturing hub in the Chinese city of Zhengzhou, which is operated by Foxconn technology group, Apple will begin manufacturing iPhone 14 in India.

4.9 Hindustan Unilever GlaxoSmithKline merger:

The merger is consistent with HUL's strategy to build a profitable and sustainable food and beverage (f&r) business in India by capitalising on the health and wellness megatrend.

References:

"3 Reasons Why FIIs Continue to Pull Money Out of India - Investing.Com India." Accessed November 25, 2022. https://in.investing.com/news/3-reasons-why-FIIs-continue-to-pull-money-out-of-india-2789695.

"Both Foreign Direct Investment FDI and Foreign Institutional Investor FII Are Related to Investment in a Country. Which One of the Following Statements Best Represents an Important Difference between the Two?" Accessed November 25, 2022. https://byjus.com/question-answer/both-foreign-direct-investment-FDI-and-foreign-institutional-investor-FII-are-related-to-investment-in/.

"Business News Today: Read Latest Business News, India Business News Live, Share Market & Economy News | The Economic Times." Accessed November 25, 2022. https://economictimes.indiatimes.com/?from=mdr.

"Difference Between FDI and FII (with Comparison Chart) - Key Differences." Accessed November 25, 2022. https://keydifferences.com/difference-between-FDI-and-FII.html.

"FDI Flows to India: Recent Trends, Challenges and Way Forward." Accessed November 25, 2022. https://www.delhipolicygroup.org/publication/policy-briefs/FDI-flows-to-india-recent-trends-challenges-and-way-forward-2225.html.

"FDI Statistics | Department for Promotion of Industry and Internal Trade | MoCI | GoI." Accessed November 25, 2022. https://dpiit.gov.in/publications/FDI-statistics.

"FDI vs. FII - Top 8 Factors to Understand Better!" Accessed November 25, 2022. https://aliceblueonline.com/antiq/beginner/difference-between-FDI-and-FII/.

"FII Buying Trends in India: With Current Resilience in Domestic, Global Markets, Will Buying Sustain? | The Financial Express." Accessed November 25, 2022. https://www.financialexpress.com/market/FII-buying-trends-in-india-with-current-resilience-in-domestic-global-markets-will-buying-sustain/2669358/.

"Foreign Direct Investment (FDI) - Overview, Benefits & Disadvantages." Accessed November 25, 2022. https://corporatefinanceinstitute.com/resources/economics/foreign-direct-investment-FDI/.

"Liberalisation of the Law Relating to Foreign Institutional Investment and Its Impact on Economic Development." Accessed November 25, 2022. https://www.legalservicesindia.com/article/689/Liberalisation-of-the-Law-relating-to-Foreign-Institutional-Investment-and-its-Impact-on-Economic-Development.html.

iPleaders. "The Legality of Foreign Institutional Investment in India," October 29, 2020. https://blog.ipleaders.in/legality-foreign-institutional-investment-india/.

CHAPTER XIV

Application of Blockchain in Financial Services

Mr. Shivam Patel; Ms. Dipika Patil; Mr. Hitesh Sharma; Mr. Raviraj Solanki;
Mr. Jatin Trivedi

1. BLOCKCHAIN DEFINED:

Blockchain is a distributed, immutable ledger that enables the recording of transactions and the tracking of assets in a business network. An asset can be tangible (a house, car, cash, or land) or intangible (a business, a patent, or a reputation) (intellectual property, patents, copyrights, branding). On a blockchain network, virtually anything of value can be tracked and traded, reducing risk and costs for all parties involved.

Importance of Blockchain:

Information drives the economy. The more quickly and accurately it is received, the better. Blockchain is ideal for delivering this information because it provides immediate, shared, and completely transparent information that is stored on an immutable ledger that can only be accessed by members of the network with the appropriate permissions. A distributed ledger network can track orders, payments, accounts, production, and more. And because members share a single view of the truth, you can see all transaction details from beginning to end, providing you with greater confidence, as well as new efficiencies and opportunities.

Key Elements of a Blockchain

1. Distributed Ledger Technology

The distributed ledger and its immutable log of transactions are accessible to all network participants. With this shared ledger, transactions are recorded only once, eliminating the effort duplication typical of conventional business networks.

2. Immutable Records

After a transaction has been recorded in the shared ledger, no participant can alter or manipulate it. If a transaction record contains an error, a new transaction must be added in order to rectify it, and both transactions must then be visible.

3. Smart Contracts

A set of rules, known as a smart contract, is stored on the blockchain and automatically executed to expedite transactions. A smart contract can define conditions for the transfer of corporate bonds, stipulate payment terms for travel insurance, and much more.

How Blockchain Works

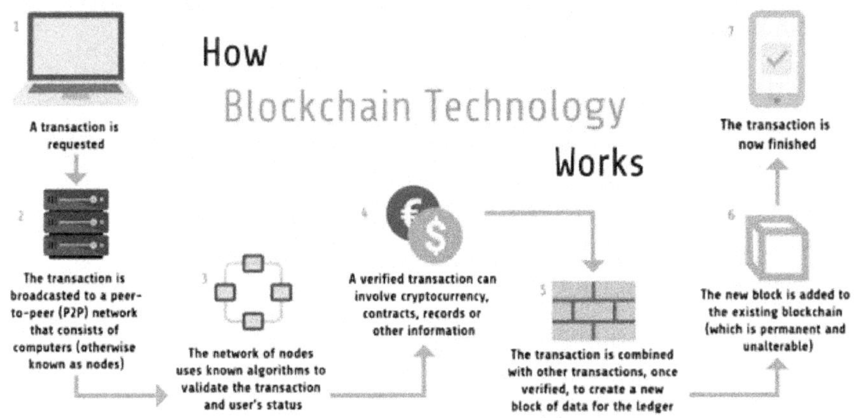

Source: How-Blockchain-Technology-works - iPleaders

1. As Each Transaction Occurs, It Is Recorded As A "Block" Of Data

These transactions represent the transfer of a tangible (a product) or intangible (a service) asset (intellectual). The data block can store the data of your choosing, including who, what, when, where, how much, and even the condition, such as the temperature of a food shipment.

2. Each Block Is Connected To The Ones Before And After It

These blocks form a data chain as an asset moves from one location to another or as ownership is transferred. The blocks verify the precise time and order of transactions, and their secure connection prevents any block from being modified or inserted between two existing blocks.

3. Transactions Are Blocked Together In An Irreversible Chain: A Blockchain

Each additional block reinforces the verification of the preceding block and, by extension, the entire blockchain. This renders the blockchain tamper-evident, delivering the immutability that is its defining characteristic. This eliminates the possibility of tampering by a malicious actor and creates a trustworthy ledger of network transactions.

Benefits of Blockchain

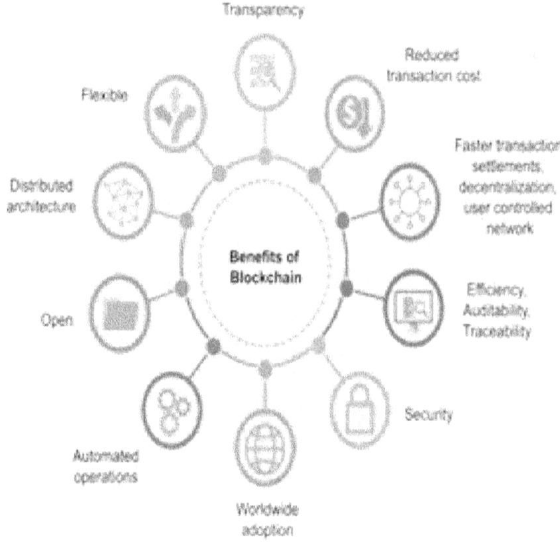

Source: Knowledge Byte: The Real Benefits of Blockchain | Cloud Credential Council

Changes Required:

Operations frequently waste time with redundant record keeping and third-party validations. Information management systems are susceptible to fraud and cyberattacks. Data verification can be impeded by a lack of transparency. With the advent of the Internet of Things, transaction volumes have exploded. All of this slows business, depletes profits, and necessitates a new approach. Introduce blockchain.

1. Greater Trust

As a member of a members-only network, you can be confident that you are receiving accurate and timely data via blockchain, and that your confidential blockchain records will only be shared with network members to whom you have granted access.

2. Greater Security

All network participants must agree on the accuracy of the data, and all validated transactions are immutable because they are recorded permanently. Even a system administrator is unable to delete a transaction.

3. More Efficiencies

A distributed ledger that is shared among network participants eliminates time-consuming record reconciliations. A set of rules, known as a smart contract, can be stored on the blockchain and executed automatically to expedite transactions.

Types Of Blockchain Networks

There are numerous methods for constructing a blockchain network. They can be public, private, permission-based, or consortium-built.

1. Public Blockchain Networks

A public blockchain is one in which anyone can join and take part, such as Bitcoin. There may be significant computational power requirements, little or no privacy for transactions, and inadequate security. These are important considerations for blockchain enterprise use cases.

2. Private Blockchain Networks

Similar to a public blockchain network, a private blockchain network is a decentralised peer-to-peer network. However, a single organisation controls who is permitted to participate, executes a consensus protocol, and maintains the distributed ledger. Depending on the use case, this can significantly increase participants' trust and confidence. A private blockchain can be deployed behind an enterprise's firewall and even hosted on-premises.

3. Permissioned Blockchain Networks

Typically, businesses that establish a private blockchain will establish a permissioned blockchain network. Notably, public blockchain networks may also be permissioned. This restricts who can participate in the network and what transactions are permitted. To join, participants must obtain an invitation or permission.

4. Consortium Blockchains

Multiple entities are able to share the responsibility of maintaining a blockchain. These preselected entities determine who may submit transactions or gain access to the data. A consortium blockchain is ideal for business transactions in which all participants must have permission and share responsibility for the blockchain.[1]

Blockchain Security

Risk Management Systems For Blockchain Networks

When developing a blockchain-based enterprise application, it is crucial to have a comprehensive security strategy that employs cybersecurity frameworks, assurance services, and best practises to reduce the risk of attacks and fraud.

Basic Blockchain Security

Blockchain technology generates a data structure with inherent security properties. It relies on cryptography, decentralisation, and consensus to ensure the integrity of transactions. In the majority of blockchains or distributed ledger technologies (DLT), the data is organised into blocks, with each block containing a single transaction or a group of transactions. Each new block in a cryptographic chain is connected to the previous blocks in such a way that it is nearly impossible to tamper with the chain. A consensus mechanism verifies and accepts all transactions within the blocks, ensuring that each transaction is valid and accurate. Blockchain technology facilitates decentralisation through the participation of network participants. There is no single point of failure, and transactions cannot be altered by a single user. However, distributed ledger technologies vary in critical security aspects.

How Security Differs By Blockchain Types

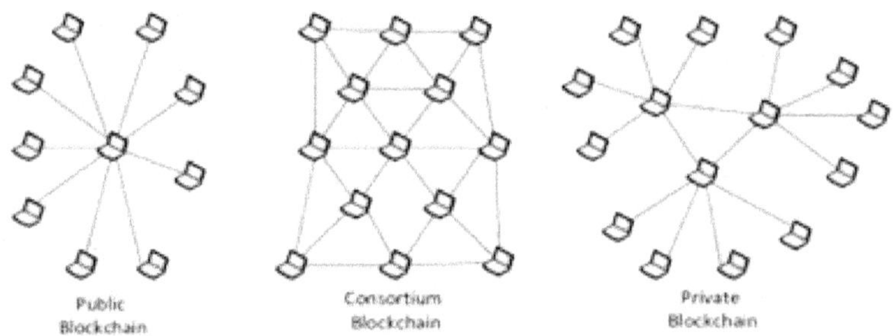

Source: K24970981119.pdf (ijitee.org)

Who can participate in Blockchain networks and who has access to the data can vary. Networks are typically labelled as public or private, indicating who is permitted to participate, and permissioned or permissionless, indicating how participants gain access.

Public and private blockchains

Typically, anyone can join a public blockchain network and participants can remain anonymous. A public blockchain relies on internet-connected computers for transaction validation and consensus formation. Bitcoin is the most well-known example of a public blockchain, and consensus is reached through "bitcoin mining." Computers on the Bitcoin network, referred to as "miners," attempt to solve a complex cryptographic problem in order to generate proof of work and thus validate the transaction. Aside from public keys, this type of network has few identity and access controls.

Private blockchains typically permit only well-known organisations to join and use identity to confirm membership and access privileges. Together, the organisations constitute a "business network" exclusive to members.

A private blockchain in a permissioned network reaches consensus via a process known as "selective endorsement," in which known users verify the transactions.

Only members with special permissions and access can manage the transaction ledger. This type of network requires increased identity and access controls. When developing a blockchain application, it is essential to determine which network type will best serve your business objectives. Private and permission-based networks can be tightly regulated and are favoured for compliance and regulatory purposes. Public and permissionless networks can achieve greater decentralisation and distribution, though.

1. **Public blockchains** are public, and anyone can join them and validate transactions.

2. **Private blockchains** are restricted and usually limited to business networks. A single entity, or consortium, controls membership.

3. **Permissionless blockchains** have no restrictions on processors.

4. **Permissioned blockchains** are limited to a select set of users who are granted identities using certificates.[2]

Financial Services

Financial services are the services provided by financial institutions. Asset Management Companies and Liability Management Companies make up the financial institutions. There are leasing companies, mutual funds, merchant bankers, and issue/portfolio managers in Asset Management Companies, whereas Liability Management Companies have bill discounting and acceptance houses.

In other words, the term "financial service" refers to the products and services that banks provide, as they offer a variety of facilities for financial transactions and other financial activities, such as loans, insurance, credit cards, investment opportunities, money management, and information on the stock market and other issues, such as market fluctuations.

This sector's primary objective is to serve as an intermediary between individual and institutional investors, thereby facilitating financial transactions.

Definition of Financial Services

The financial service industry is defined as, "The collection of organisations which intermediate and facilitate financial transactions of individual and institutional investors from their resource allocation activities through time".

Thus, the financial services comprise of various works related to change of savings into investment.

Types of Financial Services

According to the user profile, the financial services are divided into wholesale financial services and retail financial services. Wholesale financial services are services that are converted into retail products. Utilized by industry and business professionals. Individuals receive retail financial services for direct consumption. The following are the classifications of financial services:

A. Traditional Activities The historical financial intermediaries provide various services, including money and capital market activity. The traditional activities are divided into fund-based and non-fund-based categories. These are also referred to as asset-based and fee-based financial services, respectively.

1. Fund/Asset Based Financial Services Asset-based financial services are financial services that are used to create assets or are backed by assets, in which funds are converted into assets. It includes the following:

1) Lease Financing : The agreement between a lessor and a lessee is known as a lease. The lessor is the asset's owner, while the lessee is the asset's user. In this agreement, the lessor transfers an asset to the lessee for a specified period of time in exchange for regular rent. At the conclusion of the lease term, the asset is returned to the lessor until the contract is renewed.

2) Hire Purchase : The term "hire purchase" refers to the leasing of an asset for a specified period of time, followed by the subsequent purchase of the asset. At the time of asset sharing, the person renting the asset acquires ownership and is authorised to use it. As legal advice, it is used for financing capital goods such as industrial finance, financing consumer goods, and selling consumer goods on hire purchase.

3) Factoring : Factoring is performed when a business requires immediate cash. This is accomplished by selling invoices and other accounts receivable to a factor at a discount in exchange for immediate cash. This cash is required for the business to operate continuously.

4) Forfaiting : Forfaiting is the method of financing international trade receivables. It refers to the purchase of trade bills/promissory notes by banks and financial institutions in lieu of recourse against the seller. The purchase is made by applying a discount to the documents that accounts for the overall risk of nonpayment in collection. The various collection issues are the responsibility of the buyer who pays the seller in cash after discounting the bills and notes.

5) Mutual Fund : Mutual funds are a type of investment in which a pool of funds from multiple investors is used to purchase securities such as stocks, bonds, money market instruments, and other similar assets. The fund is managed by money managers who invest the fund's capital and seek capital gains and income for the fund's investors. The portfolio of a mutual fund is organised in accordance with the prospectus' stated investment objective.

6) Exchange Traded Funds (ETFs) : It is traded similarly to stocks on the stock market. It has assets such as stocks, commodities, and bonds. They trade close to the net asset value in accordance with the trading day's activities. ETFs also monitor various indexes, such as the stock index and bond index. Exchange traded funds are advantageous as investments due to their low costs, tax efficiency, and stock-like characteristics. They are extremely popular among exchange-traded securities.

7) Consumer Credit/Consumer Finance : Consumer credit refers to the activities associated with extending credit to consumers in order to enable them to acquire their own goods for daily use. Credit merchandising is also known as deferred payments, instalment purchasing, hire purchase, pay-out-of-income scheme, pay-as-you-earn scheme, easy payment, credit purchasing, instalment credit plan, etc.

8) Bill Discounting : Bill discounting or a bill of exchange is a money market instrument that is short-term, negotiable, and easily liquidiable. It is used to finance a transaction involving goods and is therefore a trade-related instrument.

9) Housing Finance : Housing finance refers to the collection of all housing-related financial arrangements offered by Housing Finance Companies (HFCs) to meet housing needs.

10) Venture Capital : There are two words in venture capital: venture and capital. Capital refers to the human and non-human resources required to launch a business, whereas venture refers to the method of doing something whose outcome is unknown and entails multiple types of loss.

2. Fee/Non-Fund Based Financial Services The fee-based financial service does not provide instantaneous funds, but rather facilitates the creation of funds. It includes the following:

1) Merchant Banking :

The merchant banker may be an individual or an institution, such as an underwriter or an agent for corporations and municipalities that allocate securities. In addition, they perform broker or dealer functions, maintain the market for previously issued securities, and offer advisory services to investors. It plays an essential role in mergers and acquisitions, private equity placements, and corporate reorganisation.

2) Credit Rating :

The credit rating is the process in which the symbol is assigned to the instrument for some special work which is referred to as benchmark of present knowledge on related capacity on the issuer to service its debt obligation on particular time. The credit rating symbols are predominantly alphabetic or numeric. Credit rating facilitates the comparison of various financial instruments. The basic objective of credit rating is to inform the investors about the relative ranking of the default-loss probability for required fixed income investment in comparison to other rated instruments.

3) Stock Broking :

The method of bringing together buyers and sellers of stocks at the stock exchange is known as stock broking. It is the role of the intermediary of financial services. It is carried out by brokers, both principal brokers and sub brokers authorised by the SEBI. The stock broker may be an individual, a brokerage firm, or a corporation.

4) Securitisation :

Securitisation is the process of transforming a person's present or future cash flows into marketable securities that can be sold. These cash inflows can be derived from financial assets such as mortgage loans, auto loans, trade receivables, credit card receivables, and fare collections, and serve as collateral for borrowing. Despite the fact that an individual can utilise securitisation instruments for effective economic growth, these instruments are not required.

5) Letters of Credit (LOC) :

A letter of credit is issued by the bank of the buyer to the seller on the basis of a written commitment to repay the cost of goods and services provided by the seller to the buyer in exchange for submitting the required documents within the precise time, place, and to the prescribed bank, as specified in the terms and conditions of the LOC.

6) Bank Guarantees :

The guarantee is the contract between the issuing bank and the client whereby the bank attempts to collect the claims presented by the client against the customer on whose behalf the bank issued the guarantee. The client may collect the payment of default from the bank if the customer fails to fulfil the obligation. The bank is only liable for the amount stated in the contract if the amount of default exceeds the total amount the bank must pay.

B. Modern Activities

In addition to traditional services, the financial intermediaries offer additional services. These are activities unrelated to funds. These fall under the category of New Financial Products and Services. The various services consist of the following:

1. It offers a variety of project advisory services, beginning with the preparation of the project report and continuing through fund-raising and obtaining the necessary government approvals.
2. The planning and implementation of the merger and acquisition process.
3. It assists corporate clients in restructuring their capital structures.
4. It serves as trustee for debenture holders.
5. It contributes to a better outcome by modifying the management structure and management style as needed.
6. It aids in identifying the best joint venture partners and drafting joint venture agreements, which aids in structuring financial collaborations and joint ventures.
7. It also aids ailing businesses by rehabilitating and reorganising the scheme's implementation plans.
8. It reduces risk by using swaps and other derivative products to mitigate exchange rate risk, interest rate risk, economic risk, and political risk.
9. It It aids in the management of the portfolio of a large public company.
10. It provides risk management services such as insurance and buy-back options.
11. It also advises clients on how to select the most advantageous source of funds, taking into account the various funds, costs, lending periods, etc.

12. It also assists the client in reducing debt costs and selecting the optimal debt-to-equity ratio.

13. It also aids companies with similar credit ratings that wish to go public by issuing debt instruments.

14. It comprises the numerous services associated with the capital market, including:

- Clearing services
- Registration and transfers
- State custody of securities
- Collection of income on securities

Regulatory Framework of Financial Services

Typically, the regulatory framework aims to establish efficient and effective financial institutions, in addition to preserving the stability of the transmission method and protecting the consumers of financial services. The regulatory structure of India's financial services is depicted below:

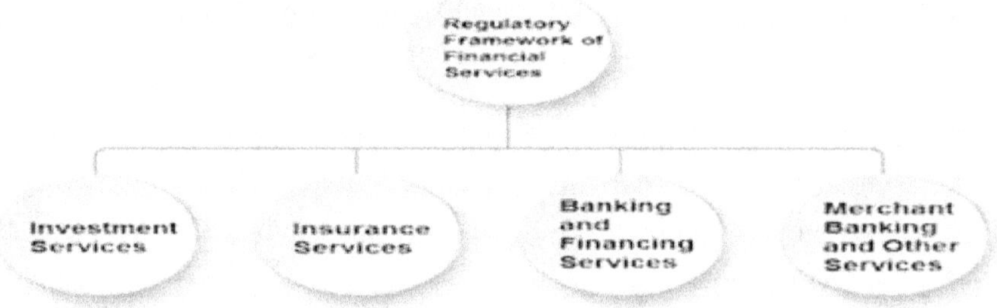

Source: Financial Services | Definition, Objectives, Scope, Types, Nature, Importance & Limitations (toppers4u.com)

1) Framework for Banking and Financing Services :

The banks perform two functions that influence their growth. These are the functions of saving and investing. The Central Government and RBI supervise the operations of the banking and financial institutions. The central government and the Reserve Bank of India assist in maintaining the required rate of economic expansion. With the aid of the RBI Act and the Banking Regulation Act, the RBI regulates all financial institutions involved in saving and capital formation. There are numerous other regulations applicable to institutions involved in capital raising and lending.

i) New Branch : It gives permissions for establishing new bank or new branch.

ii) Capital : It suggests the minimum capital, reserves and need of profit and reserves, dispersion of dividends, the amount requirement for minimum cash reserve and other liquid assets.

iii) Inspection : The proper monitoring and maintenance on the functioning of the banks.

iv) Appointment : The various appointments of Chairman and Chief Executive Officer of private banks and nominating members to the Board of Directors done.

v) Monetary Policy : The planning and implementation of monetary and credit policy for effective regulation of credit flows. Maintenance of certain amount by t deciding Cash Reserve Ratio (CRR) and Statutory Liquidity Ratio (SLR). The various treasury operations are done by the regular issue of bonds and repos.

vi) Credit Control : The various qualitative and quantitative credit control method are used for managing credit flow to different industries.

vii) Other Services : The various other services like regulating, factoring, bill discounting and credit card services are offered by the banks.

2) Framework for Insurance Services :

Prior to the nationalisation of life and general insurance, the Insurance Act of 1938 was enacted to regulate insurers. The LIC, founded in 1956, and GIC, founded in 1973, are the two largest insurance institutions. The nationalisation of insurance firms has altered the operation of the Act. The regulatory functions were inherited by LIC and GIC.

In 1996, the Insurance Regulatory Authority (IRA) was established as a result of the RBI's 1993 appointment of the Malhotra Committee to recommend ways to improve the operation of India's various insurance services.

The IRA provides the following services to both public and private insurers:

i) Orderly Growth : The regulation and promotion of the insurance business leads to the orderly growth.

ii) Exercise of Powers : The various powers and functions of the controller of Insurance under the Insurance Act, 1938, LIC Act, 1956 and the General Insurance Business (Nationalization) Act, 1972 or any other law relating to insurance in force at the time it is exercised and performed.

iii) Protecting Policy-Holders : In addition to controlling and regulating the rates, the various interests of policyholders, including the assignment of policy nomination by policyholders, insurable interest, settlement of insurance claims, surrender value of policy, and other terms and conditions of contract insurance. It is the responsibility of the insurer to safeguard advantageous terms and conditions.

iv) Professionalization : The professional organisation related to the insurance business should be controlled and promoted.

v) Information : The governing body can request various inspection, inquiry, and investigation information, including audits of insurers, insurance intermediaries, and other organisations related to the insurance industry.

vi) Books Maintenance : The way of maintaining the books of accounts with all the statements of accounts is prescribed to the insurers and other insurance intermediaries.

3) Framework for Investment Services :

Investment services are associated with various fund-based activities, such as mutual funds and venture capital. In a similar manner, the stock exchange and brokerage institution are also associated with investment activities. The rules they adhere to can be discussed with other investment endeavours. Securities Contracts (Regulation) Act of 1956 (SCRA). It is defined that SEBI Regulations and Reserve Bank of India comprise the regulatory framework.

4) Framework for Merchant Banking and Other Services :

The functioning of various types of intermediaries involved in the management of public and right issue of capital, such as merchant bankers, underwriters, brokers, market-makers, registrars, advisors, collection bankers, advertisement consultants, debenture trustees, and credit rating agencies, etc., is governed by a number of SEBI guidelines, which are described below.

- SEBI (Merchant Banker) Regulation, 1992
- SEBI Rules for Underwriters
- SEBI (Brokers and Sub-brokers) Regulation, 1992
- SEBI Rules for Registrars to an Issue and Share Transfer Agents, 1993
- SEBI (Bankers to an Issue) Regulations, 1994[3]

What are the Benefits of Blockchain in Finance?

The Ethereum blockchain enables more open, inclusive, and secure business networks, shared operating models, more efficient processes, lower costs, and the introduction of new banking and finance products and services. It enables the issuance of digital securities in shorter time frames, at lower unit costs, and with greater levels of customization. Thus, digital financial instruments can be tailored to investor preferences, thereby expanding the market for investors, reducing costs for issuers, and minimising counterparty risk. Over the past five years, the technology has matured to the point where it is suitable for enterprise use, demonstrating the following advantages:

1. Security: Its distributed consensus-based architecture eliminates single points of failure and reduces the requirement for data intermediaries such as transfer agents, messaging system operators, and inefficient monopoly utilities. Additionally, Ethereum enables the implementation of secure application code designed to be tamper-resistant against fraud and malicious third parties, making it virtually impossible to hack or manipulate.

2.Transparency: Utilizing mutualized standards, protocols, and shared processes, it serves as a single shared source of truth for network participants.

3.Trust: Its transparent and immutable ledger facilitates collaboration, data management, and agreement-making between parties in a business network.

4.Programmability: It facilitates the creation and execution of smart contracts — tamper-resistant, deterministic software that automates business logic — thereby enhancing trust and productivity.

5.Privacy: It offers market-leading tools for granular data privacy across every layer of the software stack, enabling selective data sharing in enterprise networks. This significantly enhances transparency, trust, and efficiency while maintaining privacy and secrecy.

6.High-Performance: Its private and hybrid networks are designed to support hundreds of transactions per second and periodic network traffic spikes.

7.Scalability: It enables interoperability between private and public chains, providing each enterprise solution with the mainnet's global reach, tremendous resiliency, and high integrity.

According to a report by Jupiter Research, blockchain deployments will enable banks to realise savings of up to $27 billion on cross-border settlement transactions by 2030's end, a reduction of more than 11 percent. Ethereum in particular has already demonstrated disruptive economics, generating greater than 10-fold cost advantages over incumbent technologies. Financial institutions recognise that distributed ledger technology will save banks and major financial institutions billions of dollars over the next decade.

How does the Digitization of Financial Instruments Impact Finance?

The digitization of financial instruments, which includes digital assets, smart contracts, and programmable money, extends the blockchain's benefits by establishing unprecedented levels of connectivity and programmability between products, services, assets, and holdings. These digitised instruments will redefine the processes of commercial and financial markets, establishing a new paradigm in which value is created at every point of interaction.

Digital financial instruments provide the following advantages for businesses:

1. **Authenticity And Scarcity:**

Digitization ensures data integrity and enables asset provenance and complete transaction history from a centralised source of truth.

1. **Programmable Capabilities:**

Code that addresses governance, compliance, data privacy, identity (KYC/AML attributes), system incentives, and features that manage stakeholder participation (for voting and other rights) can be embedded directly into the assets.

3. **Streamlined Processes:**

Increasing the level of automation improves overall operational effectiveness. It enables real-time settlement, auditing, and reporting, and reduces processing times, the potential for error and delay, and the number of steps and intermediaries required in traditional processes to achieve the same level of confidence.

4. **Economic Benefits:**

Processes that are automated and more efficient reduce infrastructure, operation, and transaction costs.

5. Market Reactivity:

Digital securities permit greater customization than conventional securities and can be issued in a shorter amount of time. Issuers can create digital financial instruments that correspond directly to investor demand.

6. New Products And Markets:

Secure, scalable, and rapid asset transfers, fractionalized ownership of real-world assets, tokenized microeconomies, and more are all possible with blockchain technology.

Collectively, these advantages result in more accountable and transparent governance systems, more efficient business models, enhanced incentive alignment between stakeholders, greater liquidity, lower capital costs, reduced counterparty risk, access to a broader investor and capital base, and access to all other digital financial instruments.

A. **Impact of Blockchain on the Capital markets:**

Capital markets refer to the matching of issuers with capital needs to investors with risk and return profiles that correspond. Whether issuers are entrepreneurs, startups, or large organisations, capital-raising can be difficult. Companies are confronted with increasingly stringent regulations, longer time to market, interest rate volatility, and liquidity risk. They must navigate the absence of rigorous monitoring, thorough regulation, and adequate market infrastructure for issuing, settlement, clearing, and trading, particularly in emerging markets. Blockchain offers multiple advantages for a variety of capital market applications:

- Decentralized utilities' elimination of a single point of failure
- Promotion of capital market operations reducing costs, streamlining procedures, and decreasing settlement times
- The digitization of processes and workflows, which reduces operational risks of fraud, human error, and overall counterparty risk.
- Digitization or tokenization of assets and financial instruments, rendering them programmable and considerably less difficult to manage and trade. Through enhanced connectivity and the possibility of fractionalized ownership, they gain greater market access in token form. This increases liquidity and reduces the cost of capital.

B. Importance of Blockchain on Asset Management:

There are demands for venture capital firms, private equity firms, real estate funds, and specialty markets to improve liability risk management, adopt more dynamic decision-making structures, and address the increasing complexity and ever-changing nature of regulations. The distributed ledger technology can streamline asset and stakeholder management. It permits:

- Automatic fund initiation
- Integrated engagement of stakeholders with digitised assets and services
- Portfolio and existing holdings are digitised to increase market access, liquidity, and fractionalization.
- Integrated privacy settings that can be modified for transaction confidentiality.
- Programming voting and other shareholder rights and obligations into digital assets, resulting in a seamless user experience and reduced human error risks.
- Creation and enforcement of incentive mechanisms to encourage participation and deter criminal behaviour
- Improved investor and stakeholder governance and transparency
- Efficient cap table management
- Automated fund management
- Automated transfer agency for asset administration

C. Impact of Blockchain Global Payments And Remittances:

Today, global payments and remittances are executed by a variety of intermediaries who charge fees for their services. It takes two to seven days and costs an average of 6.94 percent to send $200 internationally. In other words, fees, intermediaries, and financial institutions directly reduce remittances by $48 billion. Blockchain can streamline payment and remittance processes, significantly reducing settlement times and costs. It permits:

- Swift and secure domestic retail transactions
- Rapid and secure domestic settlement of wholesale and securities
- Rapid and secure international payments
- Gross settlement in real time between central banks, commercial banks, and independent banks.

- The digitization of KYC/AML information and transaction history reduces fraud risks and enables real-time authentication.
- Automated regulatory auditing and oversight
- Multiple payment methods enabled on the blockchain: Tokenized fiat currency, stablecoin, and digital currency

D. How Does Blockchain Impact Banking And Lending?

Transaction, loan, mortgage, and payment services constitute the core of banking. Many of these services rely on executing legacy processes. For instance, between information verification, credit scoring, loan processing, and the distribution of funds, it takes 30 to 60 days for individuals to obtain a mortgage and 60 to 90 days for small and medium-sized businesses to obtain a business loan. Blockchain can streamline banking and lending services by decreasing counterparty risk and settlement times. It permits:

- Authenticated documentation and KYC/AML data, minimising operational risks and enabling real-time financial document verification.
- Credit prediction and credit scoring markets that are instantaneously informed by the collection of user activity and sanctioned data across a network.
- Automated syndicate formation, underwriting, and disbursement of funds (principal and interest payments), reducing syndication's cost, delay, and friction.
- Because digitization enables real-time asset management, tracking, and enforcement of regulatory controls, collateralization of assets is facilitated.

E. Impact of Blockchain Trade Finance:

Trade finance refers to the infrastructure, procedures, and funding that support the supply chains of international trade. The industry continues to rely on security-vulnerable paper-based processes. Individual transactions may take up to 90-120 days due to the time required to process letters of credit, verify documents, and establish stakeholder trust. The entire trade finance lifecycle can be digitised with increased security and efficiency using blockchain technology. It can facilitate more transparent governance, shorter processing times, lower capital requirements, and a reduction in the risks of fraud, human error, and overall counterparty risk. It permits:

- Digitized and authenticated documentation (such as letters of credit and bills of lading) and KYC/AML data with real-time financial document verification.
- Asset digitization to facilitate quicker settlements
- Through the use of shared secure networks and digitalized procedures, more efficient financial structures are created.
- Creation of a consistent financing instrument for the entire trade lifecycle, eliminating the legacy practise of negotiating separate financing instruments for each phase of the trade.

F. Impact of Blockchain on Insurance:

Property and casualty insurance claims are susceptible to fraud, and claim evaluations can take considerable time. Blockchain can securely streamline data verification, claims processing, and payment disbursement, thereby significantly reducing processing time. It permits:

- Authenticated documentation and KYC/AML data, reducing the risk of fraud and easing claim evaluations.
- Claims processing automation utilising smart contracts
- Contracts with automated parameterized payouts triggered by the occurrence of a specific risk
- Automated insurance payment distribution
- Tokenized reinsurance markets will facilitate policy reinsurance in open marketplaces, displacing traditional broker and relationship-based systems.

G. Impact of Blockchain on Compliance:

Regulatory compliance has grown in importance in the business and finance sectors. It is necessary in order to ensure that financial institutions adhere to all applicable laws, rules, and regulations. It is extremely difficult for businesses to keep up with the rapidity and complexity of regulatory change, especially when they operate internationally and are thus subject to multiple regulatory regimes. Blockchain provides these advantages:

- Programming unique governance and compliance attributes into digital assets
- Streamlined, real-time processes that automate data verification and reporting, facilitate regulatory oversight, reduce operational friction, and

eliminate errors associated with manual auditing and other activities.

- Implementation of incentive structures to enhance network governance.[4]

References:

"Blockchain in Finance & Fintech: The Future of Financial Services | ConsenSys." Accessed November 21, 2022. https://consensys.net/blockchain-use-cases/finance/.

"Financial Services | Definition, Objectives, Scope, Types, Nature, Importance & Limitations." Accessed November 21, 2022. https://www.toppers4u.com/2022/02/financial-services-definition.html.

"What Is Blockchain Security? | IBM." Accessed November 21, 2022. https://www.ibm.com/topics/blockchain-security.

"What Is Blockchain Technology? - IBM Blockchain | IBM." Accessed November 21, 2022. https://www.ibm.com/in-en/topics/what-is-blockchain.

Endnotes:

[1] "What Is Blockchain Technology? - IBM Blockchain | IBM."

[2] "What Is Blockchain Security? | IBM."

[3] "Financial Services | Definition, Objectives, Scope, Types, Nature, Importance & Limitations."

[4] "Blockchain in Finance & Fintech: The Future of Financial Services | ConsenSys."

CHAPTER XV

Impact of Russia-Ukraine Conflict on Indian Economy

Ms. Sakshi Singh; Ms. Janvi Mistry; Ms. Srushti Patel; Mr. Jay Modi; Mr. Deep Shah

Introduction:

The war between the two neighbouring countries Russia and Ukraine is a major setback for the global economy, as it has a negative impact on growth and the inflation rate. As a result of this crisis, the global economy will experience slower growth and higher inflation. Russia and Ukraine are the two largest producers of commodities, especially oil. Certainly, the war would cause an increase in global prices. Wheat, of which Ukraine and Russia produce 30 percent of global exports, has pushed up food prices. The petroleum importers with the greatest impact on current accounts will be ASEAN economies, India, frontier economies, and some Pacific island economies. As a result of the Ukraine conflict, the majority of Indians are reducing their consumption of fried foods and even vegetables. Since the conflict between Russia and Ukraine erupted, oil companies have raised their prices, causing consumers to feel the pinch. Due to this, diesel, gasoline, and vegetable oils become prohibitively expensive.

On February 24, 2022, Russia and Ukraine engaged in a conflict that has affected the Indian economy, resulting in repercussions and effects in various areas and facets. In a meeting of the United Nations (UN), India abstained from voting. India has taken a neutral stance at the United Nations meeting. It has been forty days since the beginning of this conflict. Let's discuss a few key aspects of the Russia-Ukraine conflict and its impact on India and its economy.

1. Immediate Adversities:

a. As the conflict broke out, the Sensex fell by 2700 points due to panic selling and investor anxiety, resulting in the loss of Rs. 7.5 lakh crores from the stock market. The Russian stock market plummeted by fifty percent, which had a profound effect on all Asian stock markets. The conflict also contributed to the near-record gold and crude oil prices, which we will discuss further.

b. According to the SBI report, India has limited banking and corporate sector ties with both countries, so the impact will be minimal in these areas. The majority of the non-Russian organisations that ceased operations in Russia were American or affiliated with the United States, including PayPal, McDonald's, Disney, etc.

2. Crude Oil & Gold Prices:

a. Russia is one of the world's largest crude oil producers, and as a result of the sanctions imposed by the United States on Russia, crude oil prices are anticipated to rise further as a result of the ongoing tensions. The sanctions may also result in a rise in crude oil prices, which have already surpassed $100 per barrel ($108 as of 5th May, 2022) for the first time in 14 years, and have risen by 45 percent in the first six months of 2021 (rising to $80 per barrel). However, there will be a negligible impact on India as it imports the majority of its oil requirements, the majority of which comes from the Middle East due to the geographical proximity of the countries. Russia has a vast area from which it can ship oil by pipeline to Europe and neighbouring countries, by road to countries in the south of Russia, and by sea route to countries in the west via Alaska.

b. Additionally, gold prices rose to $2,000 per ounce. During the conflict, the equity market became volatile, prompting many investors to switch from equity and other investments to gold, which is regarded as a safe haven in such circumstances. These market sentiments also contributed to the rise in gold prices and the decline in the equity and other markets.

c. On March 30, Russia also decided to peg the ruble to gold, with 1 gramme of gold equaling 5,000 rubles until June 30, 2022. Consequently, the Russian ruble has already regained its lost value, and there is a good chance that its value will continue to rise. As the ruble regains its value, Russia may also increase its gold supply, which could further strengthen the ruble. Russia is the third largest gold supplier in the world and could easily increase its gold supply. If the value of the ruble increases significantly, the demand for the U.S. dollar may decrease, as it will be more expensive to buy gold in dollars than in rubles, and people may shift from dollars to rubles.

3. Higher Inflation:

a. Due to this ongoing conflict, gasoline and diesel prices have already reached an all-time high. Prices of commodities in India are heavily influenced by the cost of gasoline and diesel. When the price of gasoline and diesel is increased, transportation and logistics costs will also rise, leading to an increase in the cost of both domestic and international goods. The price of oil is anticipated to increase further. As India imports approximately 80% of its oil requirements, this will have a negative impact on the country. From Russia, India imports $205 billion worth of oils and minerals, $832 million worth of precious stones, and $609 million worth of fertilisers, so an increase in the prices of these commodities could cause India to experience significant inflation.

b. Russia provides crude oil, natural gas, and other resources to the majority of Europe. Russia is one of the world's largest wheat producers and accounts for more than 18 percent of international exports. India imports 84 percent of its sunflower oil from Russia. If all of these supply chains are disrupted, it will have a significant negative impact, leading to inflation and other circumstances.

4. Favourable movements on commodities which India exports:

a. Russia and Ukraine are two of the world's largest grain producers and exporters, but due to the current conflict, grain exports have been halted and a market shortage is a distinct possibility. For example, Russia and Ukraine are two of the leading wheat producers on the market, but the supply of wheat is being disrupted as a result of the war. India is already filling this void by increasing wheat exports.

b. Wheat from Gujarat, Rajasthan, and Uttar Pradesh is now being delivered at a price of Rs 2,400 to Rs 2,450 per quintal, compared to Rs 2,100 per quintal or so, and in a mere 15 days. The only factor to consider is that the Indian government must carefully manage both domestic stock availability and exports. Additionally, the prices of edible oil, vegetable oil, and oilseeds are skyrocketing.

c. The mustard oil farmers of Rajasthan and Uttar Pradesh, who are preparing to sell their harvests in the coming weeks, may also be eligible for a financial reward. Current mustard prices exceed Rs. 6,500 per quintal, which is higher than the minimum support price of Rs. 5,050 per quintal. Because synthetic fibre is becoming more expensive, cotton costs have also increased. Brent crude oil is a significant factor in the price increases of the aforementioned commodities and others. India must carefully observe and analyse the current situation, and act accordingly, so that this ongoing conflict may have a favourable outcome in many of these areas.

[1]

5. Potential Opportunities for India:

a. During this conflict, the United States and its numerous allies decided to end their operations in Russia. SWIFT (Society for Worldwide Interbank Financial Telecommunications) is an international organisation that is connected to more than 200 countries and 11000+ banks worldwide, processed over 4 crore transactions per day, and decided to cut ties with Russia.

b. This situation has created a void that can be filled by India's own UPI (Unified Payments Interface). In the past few years, UPI usage has increased dramatically, and UPI has evolved to the point where digital payments can be made even without an internet connection. In fiscal year 21-22, UPI transactions surpassed $1 Trillion. If UPI is able to fill this void and replace SWIFT in the Russian market, it will be a huge step forward for India in the financial sector.

c. Nepal also adopted UPI for P2P payments, thereby facilitating the expansion of its businesses. NPCI (National Payments Corporation of India) must onboard as many individuals and banks as quickly as possible because India must become a superpower without relying primarily on its military. In addition, the RuPay card was recently introduced in Nepal, following Bhutan, Singapore, and the United Arab Emirates. If India takes this to a higher level and on a larger scale, it may be able to capture similar markets in larger nations such as Russia.

d. As a result of the host nation's determination to make the sanctions as painful as possible, Russia's aviation industry is also paralysed, as a large number of aircrafts may be subject to lease agreements that may be terminated or insurance coverage may be halted. India could aid its ally by establishing itself in such industries, leading to an increase in foreign exchanges and revenues from such operations.

6. Impact on stock market

Since the outbreak of the crisis, India's financial markets have been extremely volatile. The BSE Sensex dropped more than 1,250 points in early trade on Tuesday, reaching a session low of 56,394, while the rupee fell 33 paise, or 0.44 percent, to 74.84 per dollar.

According to Siddhartha Khemka, Head-Retail Research at Motilal Oswal Financial Services, domestic equities fell sharply on Tuesday, mirroring the weakness in global markets due to the ongoing escalation between Russia and Ukraine.

Nifty gapped down below the critical 17,000 level and continued to experience selling pressure. Nevertheless, during the final hour of trading, the market recovered from lower levels and reduced its daily losses. Despite the recovery, the Nifty closed with a loss of 114 points at 17,092 for the fifth consecutive trading session. Due to the rapid escalation of the Russia-Ukraine conflict, market volatility has increased. There is no immediate resolution in sight. Moreover, rising oil prices have added to the market's pessimism. In addition, FNO monthly expiration on Thursday would maintain market volatility. Nifty managed to close above the critical level of 17,000 for the time being. In the last month, 16,800 has been a key support level for the market. In the near future, however, global weakness and consistent FII selling could add to the pressure.[2]

India's position on the consequences of the Russia-Ukraine War:

The Russian invasion of Ukraine is distinct from the numerous ongoing conflicts in other parts of the world, such as in Arab nations, Africa, or between India and China. Russia, a military superpower, has decided to invade Ukraine, which is partially supported by the United States and NATO. While the latter have stated repeatedly that they will not send troops to defend Ukraine, they have imposed severe sanctions on Russia and its leaders. These will have long-lasting effects. Due to the ongoing pandemic, new elements will be introduced into the "new normal" that the world was headed towards. Long-term and immediate national and international repercussions will result. The issues will be political and economic, and they will be interconnected. Given that many countries are directly and indirectly involved in the conflict, the international situation dictates the repercussions. Within this context, the implications for India and its people can be comprehended. War has immediate effects on international trade, capital flows, financial markets, and technology access. Rich countries' sanctions against Russia will not stop the war, and little will change in the near future. Relations between the two sides on the political and economic fronts will reveal the true impact over time. Almost certainly, the Cold War of the 1950s will resurface between an Eastern Bloc composed of Russia and China and Western powers and their allies. Since the world is significantly more interconnected than it was in the 1950s, the impact will be greater. Due to the fact that the two blocs already existed in the 1950s and there is now a sudden major disruption, it will be even worse.

- **International short run:**

Sanctions on both sides will affect trade immediately. Due to the pandemic, exports and imports will suffer, and existing supply bottlenecks will worsen. The Western powers will likely insist that other countries cease trade with Russia. For example, they will demand that other nations cease importing energy from Russia and threaten sanctions against nations and businesses that continue to trade with Russia. This would include China; otherwise, sanctions against Russia would be ineffective. Since China is the largest trading partner for many of the world's wealthiest nations, this will severely disrupt trade and cause additional supply bottlenecks. To prevent prices from skyrocketing and disrupting the global economy, the U.S. may increase the supply of petroleum products and request that friendly OPEC nations do the same. Ukraine is a major exporter of agricultural goods, and disruptions to their supplies will lead to an increase in food prices. Inasmuch as Russia and China provide a portion of the essential supplies, the trend of rising commodity prices will continue. As a result, inflation will accelerate globally, impacting people's purchasing power and weakening demand, which was already affected by the pandemic. With liquidity at a high level due to quantitative easing during the pandemic, inflation can accelerate rapidly. This will slow global economic growth.

As a result of the desire of many nations to invest domestically rather than abroad, global capital flows will decline. Together, this and the sanctions on financial flows will have an effect on the financial markets. In addition to this factor, the stock markets will decline due to heightened global uncertainty and the likely end of quantitative easing by Central Banks in the face of rising inflation and rising interest rates. All of this will have a negative effect on private investments.

- **International long run:**

The pandemic pushed the world toward a "new normal" that is likely to contain novel elements as a result of increased deglobalization and increased competition between the two blocs. There will be an increase in mistrust between the major nations on both sides, and cooperation on global issues will decline. Already, the pandemic had sown discord, with some nations suspecting that the coronavirus was intentionally spread or leaked from a laboratory. Hawks and the right wing will ascend to power. Given the strength of China's economy and Russia's technological prowess, the cold war will not be fought between vastly unequal blocs, as was the case during the 1950s. Therefore, it could be potentially more dangerous. Globally, the rich nation's bloc will not be viewed as a dependable ally because the United States recently abandoned its allies in Afghanistan and has now abandoned Ukraine. With two relatively equal blocs competing for influence in developing nations, the latter may acquire a greater degree of independence. But there is also the risk of managed regime changes, which can destabilise nations and exacerbate internal conflict. This will accelerate the rise of authoritarian governments.

Current efforts to freeze the assets of Russians in Western banks and cut off credit to their companies would compel them to develop an alternative dollar-free international payment system. Companies that defy Western sanctions, such as the Chinese, will also require such a payment system. Thus, two economic and trading blocs will emerge. The Chinese and Russians have sufficient foreign exchange reserves and a trade surplus to successfully form a bloc. All of this will have uncertain repercussions. As a result of deglobalization and a greater need for investment in home countries, global capital flows are likely to decline, with less money flowing to developing nations. This may be partially offset by the decreased flow of capital from wealthy nations to China. However, by offering more concessions, multinational corporations will force the developing world to compete for capital. This will be detrimental to the workers' interests. As militarisation increases, the military industrial complex will be bolstered worldwide. As more and more weapons are consumed in conflicts and offered to countries, the profits of these companies will increase. Producing more weapons is analogous to creating machines to destroy them in order to produce more. This will aid in overcoming the shortage of demand in the global economy and increase employment. With a greater investment in armaments, there will be a dearth of advanced technology for civilian use, which will reduce economic growth, increase inflation, and reduce investment in social sectors. All of this will worsen poverty despite the increase in employment. As workers are marginalised and capital generates greater profits, inequality will increase further. Research and development expenditures will increase, and technology companies will perform even better than during the pandemic. Deglobalization and production in the home countries will have a negative impact on the exports of traditional companies producing intermediate technology goods in developing nations.

- **National considerations:**

India will be confronted with a difficult situation in the near and distant future as a result of these perplexing events and global unpredictability. Fuel and food price increases will have an immediate effect on India's inflation, which is already at a high level. As sanctions and the war situation exacerbate supply bottlenecks, other prices will also increase. The uncertainty will deteriorate the investment climate. The decline in capital flows into the country will further depress the stock markets. The P/E ratio already dominated at high levels, so such a significant shock was bound to affect stock prices.

It is likely that the demand for gold will increase, leading to a rise in gold imports. This, coupled with the high cost of petroleum products, will result in a rise in import costs. Exports are likely to be impacted by the slowdown in global economic growth and deglobalization. As capital flows decline, the already deteriorating Balance of Payments will deteriorate further. As a result, the rupee will weaken against the dollar, which will exacerbate inflation. All of these factors, uncertainty, demand, investment, inflation, and BOP, will reduce the growth rate of the pandemic-ravaged economy.

Long-term, India will need to restructure its international relations in light of the new Cold War scenario, particularly in light of its relations with China. This is India's principal concern, not Ukraine. During the past two years, when confronting Chinese obstinacy, we have received only lip service from Western powers and radio silence from Russia. Due to the impact of deglobalization on global growth, trade, capital, and technology flows, India will need to strengthen its economy on its own. The public sector will have to play a significant role, as the private sector will be incapable of boosting itself when demand is low. The nation will need to strengthen its research and development, which will necessitate reorganising its education system and abandoning the disastrous NEP, which substituted teachers with technology. In reality, regardless of how good a policy is, if the environment is not conducive to change, it will not result in reform, and the NEP merely reinforces the existing environment. Social sectors must be given a much higher priority in order to increase worker productivity and improve their deteriorating living conditions. This will not only provide a market for the growth of the Indian economy, but it will also strengthen the nation. India would have to resist the temptation of its leaders to become more authoritarian, as doing so would drain the nation's resources.[3]

Conclusion:

The Russia-Ukraine conflict is a significant blow to the global economy and has created uncertainty in global trade; it has a significant impact on crude oil, cooking oil, and other commodities such as wheat and corn. They are the world's largest suppliers and exporters of wheat, edible oil, and other commodities. Thus, the conflict between Russia and Ukraine has a negative impact on the supplies of these commodities, particularly wheat and crude oil. It is noted that Russia and Ukraine are the world's largest suppliers of wheat and cooking oil, accounting for one-fourth of global exports. Consequently, the conflict between Russia and Ukraine has a significant impact on the Indian economy. Consequently, prices for cooking oil, gasoline, and crude oil have increased. Nevertheless, in light of the supply disruptions that have led to the skyrocketing prices of cooking oil and fuel across the globe, the international community must intervene, resolve the ongoing conflict through peaceful negotiations, and rescue the global economy, particularly the developing economies.

References:

Indian Titans Belts as Ukraine War Drives Up Prices of Necessities published in The Hindu on 24 March, 2022.

IMF blog- how War Ukraine is Reverberating Across World's Regions – Alfred – Kammar March 2022.Im

How Will the Russia- Ukraine War Impact the Indian Economy – Mimansa Verma - financial Economy 15 March 2022.

The Breach, Ukraine's, territorial integrity and the Budapest Memorandum Budjeryn, Mariana, 6 March 2022.

How Russia's war in Ukraine Rocked the Global Economy-The Economic Times 23 March, 2022.

https://bfsi.economictimes.indiatimes.com/amp/news/industry/how-will-russia-ukraine-crisis-impact-indias-economy-and-stock-market/

89762619

https://www.thehindu.com/news/international/explained-the-effects-of-the-russia-ukraine-conflict-on-the-global-economy/article65312083.ece

Endnotes:

[1] "Impact of Russia-Ukraine Conflict on Indian Economy," accessed November 25, 2022, https://taxguru.in/corporate-law/impact-russia-ukraine-conflict-indian-economy.html.

[2] www.ETBFSI.com, "How Will Russia-Ukraine Crisis Impact India's Economy and Stock Market? - ET BFSI," ETBFSI.com, accessed November 25, 2022, https://bfsi.economictimes.indiatimes.com/news/industry/how-will-russia-ukraine-crisis-impact-indias-economy-and-stock-market/89762619.

[3] "What India Needs To Do To Deal With the Consequences of the Russia-Ukraine War," accessed November 25, 2022, https://thewire.in/economy/india-russia-ukraine-war-consequences-impact.

9 798888 591627